THE STANDARDS-BASED DIGITAL SCHOOL LEADER PORTFOLIO

Using TaskStream, LiveText, and PowerPoint

Second Edition

Gregory M. Hauser
Dennis W. Koutouzos

Rowman & Littlefield Education
A division of
Rowman & Littlefield Publishers, Inc.
Lanham • New York • Toronto • Plymouth, UK
2010

Published by Rowman & Littlefield Education
A division of Rowman & Littlefield Publishers, Inc.
A wholly owned subsidiary of The Rowman & Littlefield Publishing Group, Inc.
4501 Forbes Boulevard, Suite 200, Lanham, Maryland 20706
http://www.rowmaneducation.com

Estover Road, Plymouth PL6 7PY, United Kingdom

Copyright © 2010 by Gregory M. Hauser and Dennis W. Koutouzos

All rights reserved. No part of this book may be reproduced in any form or by any electronic or mechanical means, including information storage and retrieval systems, without written permission from the publisher, except by a reviewer who may quote passages in a review.

British Library Cataloguing in Publication Information Available

Library of Congress Cataloging-in-Publication Data

Hauser, Gregory M., 1953-
  The standards-based digital school leader portfolio : using taskstream, livetext, and powerpoint / Gregory M. Hauser, Dennis W. Koutouzos.—2nd ed.
       p. cm.
  Includes bibliographical references.
  ISBN 978-1-60709-295-7 (hardcover : alk. paper)—ISBN 978-1-60709-296-4 (pbk. : alk. paper)—ISBN 978-1-60709-297-1 (ebook)
 1. Portfolios in education—Computer-aided design—Handbooks, manuals, etc. 2. School administrators—United States—Handbooks, manuals, etc.
I. Koutouzos, Dennis W., 1941- II. Title.
  LB1029.P67H38 2011
  371.2'011—dc22
                                                                    2010018376

∞™ The paper used in this publication meets the minimum requirements of American National Standard for Information Sciences—Permanence of Paper for Printed Library Materials, ANSI/NISO Z39.48-1992.

Printed in the United States of America.

CONTENTS

Acknowledgments	v
Foreword	vii
Introduction	xiii
1 Technology and School Leaders	1
2 History of the Standards-Based Digital School Leader Portfolio	15
3 Development of the Standards-Based Digital School Leader Portfolio	29
4 Digital Format Options	41
5 The PowerPoint Option	55
6 The TaskStream Option	61
7 The LiveText Option	83
8 Evaluation of the Standards-Based Digital School Leader Portfolio	103
References	109
About the Authors	115

ACKNOWLEDGMENTS

This text was the result of the generous assistance of numerous colleagues. We extend our appreciation for the generous help and support from TaskStream and in particular Aitken Thompson, chief operating officer; Webster Thompson, executive vice president; and Alex Chickosky, mentoring services associate. We also thank the staff at LiveText, and in particular, Chris Kalmus, president; Jennifer Anderson, implementation coordinator; and Sheetal Patel for their encouragement and generous support. We also thank the staff at Rowman & Littlefield for their interest and their support of this project and in particular Tom Koerner, vice president and editorial director, and Maera Stratton, editorial acquisitions. A special note of thanks is extended to Tom Thomas, a faculty colleague at Roosevelt University, for his invaluable editorial assistance. Finally, we thank the hundreds of master's and doctoral students over the years for their feedback on the various versions of the standards-based digital school leader portfolio template and tools.

We also extend credit here to the Interstate School Leaders Licensure Consortium (ISLLC 2008). Standards were developed by the Council of Chief State School Officers (CCSSO) and member states. Copies may be downloaded from the Council's Web site at www.ccsso.org.

Copyright 2008 by the Council of Chief State School Officers. Reprinted by permission of the Council of Chief State School Officers.

The images of the LiveText Web site and all associated marks and copyrights as well as the LiveText trademark are used with permission from LiveText, Inc. Copyright 1997–2009. All rights reserved.

The images of the TaskStream Web site and all associated marks and copyrights as well as the TaskStream trademark are used with permission from TaskStream, LLC. "Advancing Educational Excellence." Copyright 2002–2009. All rights reserved.

The NETS-A 2009 standards are the property of the International Society for Technology in Education (ISTE), 800-336-5191 (United States and Canada) or 541-302-3777 (Int'l), iste@iste.org, www.iste.org. Reprinted with permission. Reprint permission does not constitute endorsement by ISTE. All rights reserved.

All of the Web addresses used in this book where current at the time of publishing. Their accuracy over time cannot be ensured.

FOREWORD

The standards-based digital portfolio is an academic and performance measure for collecting the work of an aspiring educational leader. Whether a student has aspirations to become a principal, superintendent, teacher, director of technology, department head, curriculum director, or other school leader, the challenge for preparation programs in educational administration is to provide a quality learning experience. The quality of the learning experience in educational leadership preparation, however, has been a lament of critics going back to the earliest days of the field. Leadership preparation in school administration has been the subject of scrutiny since the first programs were developed in the early twentieth century.

The Levine (2005) study is an often-cited contemporary report condemning the field for its lack of rigor and quality control to ensure that schools turn out well-prepared graduates. It is representative of the kind of criticism leveled at educational leadership preparation programs as they graduated students with advanced degrees to lead our nation's schools. Yet, the field is changing to address its shortcomings, not because of the critics, but because there is a base of knowledge that informs the profession about how programs can best deliver on the goal of training quality graduates to lead our nation's schools. This book explains how educational administration programs can, in part, move closer to that goal.

In the past fifteen years the field of educational administration has taken a critical look at what K–12 leaders must *know* and *do* in order to be successful as instructional leaders. The effort by the profession to cast a critical eye *on the profession* has resulted in evolving and ongoing improvements to educational leadership training and preparation. Within the past fifteen years the field of educational administration has been on a path of reform. However, it has not been a reform event but rather a reform process. It may not have been the smoothest or straightest path, but the journey has led to incremental change and reform in how programs train future school leaders.

A contemporary reform included the dissemination of the Interstate Leaders Licensure Consortium Standards (see ISLLC 1996 and the revised ISLLC 2008 standards; Council of Chief State School Officers, 1996, 2008). The development of educational leadership standards "provided the best avenue to allow diverse stakeholders to drive improvement efforts along a variety of fronts—licensure, program approval and candidate assessment" (Council of Chief State School Officers, 1996, p. 7).

Although the dissemination of these standards generated a debate about their efficacy and relevancy in the real world of day-to-day schooling, they also generated a systematic and focused review of curricula, content, and delivery of leadership preparation programs. What the field initially responded to was a set of standards that narrowed and defined a curriculum. What the field did, however, was alter the delivery of its curriculum to address *how the content was delivered and how it was assessed*. The standards, as would soon be discovered, were only one aspect of the discussion about leadership preparation.

A significant change in educational leadership preparation came about when accreditation bodies—National Council for Accreditation of Teacher Education, in particular—and state departments of education began requiring assessment of student progress in higher education programs. Higher education's own move toward continuous improvement added momentum to a broader educational commitment to track, compile, and utilize student and organizational data. The standards became more than one-dimensional, stand-alone statements about leadership when these organizations began requiring the collection of student data.

What accreditation bodies, state departments of education, and program review processes required was more than a wink and nod to the implementation of national leadership standards. The expectation was that these standards would "play out at the preparation program level by establishing performance expectations" that were integrated within a process that led to "candidate assessment, and accountability" (Council of Chief State School Officers, 2008, p. 11). Standards became the front door through which programs in educational administration made curricular change that included behaviors which translated into practice. Evidence of student performance required student and program assessment that could document the quality of student learning as well as the preparation program itself.

In the past fifteen years, the field of educational administration has generated three significant trends related to program preparation:

1. Standards were developed and adopted as expectations within the leadership program of study within the United States;
2. Performance behaviors for aspiring school leaders became an accepted requirement and expectation within the leadership preparation curriculum;
3. Assessment of knowledge and performance behaviors that had a direct application to the day-to-day operation of a school or school district were integrated into the leadership preparation curriculum to measure quality of student outcomes.

Educational leadership programs have been leveraged by these changes to revise a curriculum around evidence of knowledge and displays of skill, ability, and behavior in fulfilling the roles and responsibilities of teacher leader, principal, superintendent, and other leadership roles within K–12 schools.

ASSESSMENT OF LEARNING IN EDUCATIONAL LEADERSHIP PREPARATION

Preparation programs have revised a curriculum that now requires a measurement of performance behavior. Assessment has become a meaningful learning experience rather than a static event in the matriculation of students through a course of study. Learning in educational leadership has moved—transitioned is perhaps a more accurate description—beyond paper and pencil tests and essays to a collection of artifacts, reports, multimedia presentations, PowerPoint shows, podcasts, and performance activities that reflect an accrual of knowledge and experience directly related to the day-to-day role of educational leader. The challenge to programs has been to capture student performance as a measure of skill and ability rather than simply require a traditional exam or term paper.

The thesis as an end-of-program summation of knowledge and learning has been supplemented, and in some cases supplanted, by a compilation of projects, papers, and assignments that reflect a student's progress through a program of study. Completion of a portfolio has become an accepted end-of-program assessment of student work and closure to a course of study in educational administration. The portfolio has become an indicator of academic preparation about leadership as well as performance evidence that a prospective principal, superintendent, or other aspiring school leader knows about and can do the day-to-day work of facilitating a school improvement meeting, planning a budget, or supervising classroom instruction. There is evidence of educational leadership by documenting the student's skill set.

The three-ring binder portfolio is transitioning from paper to online, digital, and multimedia. Hauser and Koutouzos have outlined and explained how the digital component of a portfolio can be an extension of educational leadership standards and become an integral component of teaching and learning within the educational administration curriculum. A standards-based portfolio, Hauser and Koutouzos explain,

> is an authentic assessment tool used by school leaders and school leader candidates to demonstrate intellectual accomplishment. The criteria for assessing the portfolio—construction of knowledge, disciplined inquiry, and value beyond school—are in the context of professional standards. (2005, p. 2)

The digital component of the student's portfolio is how the educational leadership program has implemented a structure to address the quality of a student's preparation. In so doing, it has improved the educational administration curriculum by creating authentic, relevant, and documented evidence of student knowledge, skill, and ability. Digital portfolios not only increase a student's use and understanding of technology, but capture performance and behavior that can be viewed as video and audio podcasts of authentic work throughout a program of study that can be easily saved, retrieved at any time, and sent to faculty members, students, and prospective employers. It is the process of documenting performance activities as well as academic learning that elevates knowledge acquisition beyond the traditional paper or test.

The standards-based digital portfolio is a component of the quality and accountability movement that is moving the training of educational leadership candidates to higher levels of knowledge, skill, and ability. Though the critics of educational leadership preparation can always find points of failure, shortcomings, and incomplete knowledge, there must also be recognition and understanding that the field has moved forward in ways that address quality of learning outcomes for educational leadership preparation. Hauser and Koutouzos have helped map out a direction for not only moving the educational administration curriculum forward, but a process to document the quality of student outcomes—for students and programs—through a standards-based digital portfolio.

James Berry, Professor of Educational Administration,
Eastern Michigan University,
Executive Director, National Council of
Professors of Educational Administration (NCPEA)

INTRODUCTION

Although there are a host of resource handbooks available to assist educators in the development of digital portfolios, few are devoted exclusively to school leaders. In response to this void in the literature, this newly revised and expanded handbook is designed to serve as a guide for school leaders in the field, educational leadership faculty, and school leader candidates in the development and use of standards-based digital school leader portfolios.

A number of issues associated with the design and use of a standards-based digital portfolio warrant special consideration by educational leadership faculty. Deciding how to incorporate a standards-based digital school leader portfolio into the curriculum requires consideration of four major factors: hardware, software, faculty, and pedagogy.

The hardware issues involve establishing standards to ensure that those who need access to the digital portfolio can access it with the least amount of difficulty. Educational leadership faculty are advised to establish hardware configurations for the creation of digital portfolios by school leader candidates. Often this decision is made easier if the institution has already established hardware and software standards.

If hardware and software standards are not clearly established, educational leadership faculty and school leader candidates will likely experience hardware and software incompatibility issues. One possible strategy to address this issue is to use the hardware and software standards of the the college or university. In this way, school leader candidates will be able to access the designated hardware and software configuration without additional cost.

Careful consideration should be given related to the training needs of educational leadership faculty using the software and hardware described in this text. Educational leadership faculty who extensively use technology in their courses will likely experience little difficulty in the incorporation of the standards-based digital school leader portfolio described in this text. Other educational leadership faculty may need additional training.

Training of faculty can be accomplished by the technology support staff—"in-house" trainers—if hardware and software standards are consistent with those of the institution. In addition, the Web-based software providers used in this text, TaskStream and LiveText, have support staff available by voice and e-mail for technical assistance. TaskStream and LiveText also have a variety of manuals and online tutorials that are useful for training purposes. The templates and samples in this text could provide a useful framework for a workshop to train educational leadership faculty.

A special concern relates to the training of adjunct faculty. Unless adjunct faculty members teach regularly in the program, they may not be as proficient as their full-time colleagues in the use of the hardware and software used in the development of the digital portfolio. If the standards-based digital school leader portfolio is implemented across the curriculum, these staff training issues become more complicated given the number of faculty needing training. As an alternative, the faculty training issues may be minimized by incorporating the standards-based digital school leader portfolio into the practicum sequence, thus only requiring training of the faculty who teach these courses.

Over the years, there have been a variety of ways in which portfolios have been incorporated into the educational leadership curriculum. In recent years, portfolios have increasingly been standards based and digital in format. The standards-based digital portfolio may be included in each course in the educational leadership curriculum, in just the practicum sequence of courses, or in lieu of the comprehensive examination.

Using the digital portfolio process can affect pedagogy in a number of ways. First, it can stimulate faculty to be more flexible and creative in designing course assignments. When assignments have the potential to become part of a portfolio in addition to being a way to exhibit competence in a course, both faculty and students view those assignments differently. Using the portfolio process can stimulate faculty to reassess individual courses and the total curriculum in light of this approach to authentic assessment. Also, the digital format could stimulate faculty creativity in the delivery of content and in course assignments.

Second, the portfolio process will encourage educational leadership faculty to evaluate the curriculum and ensure that courses provide experiential projects, activities, and artifacts appropriate for the development of a portfolio.

Third, research suggests that portfolio assessment will likely increase the volume of faculty–student communication as well as change the content of that communication if reflection and feedback are used in the portfolio process.

Fourth, if the portfolio is used across the curriculum, faculty can anticipate having a richer and fuller insight into how each course and the entire curriculum prepare school leader candidates to meet professional standards. The portfolio process could thus become an element of program evaluation.

Fifth, faculty involved in distance learning may discover the convenience and logistical advantages of the portfolio process in digital format over the conventional paper format.

Sixth, faculty will have the opportunity to develop higher level technology skills. Educational leadership faculty members who have used digital portfolios in the curriculum comment favorably regarding their own proficiency using various hardware and software.

Finally, there is an acute need for educational leadership faculty to better prepare school leaders for their responsibilities associated with technology in schools. Unfortunately, many educational leadership curricula are lacking in this area. "Looking closely at principal preparation programs at our universities, the role of the principal as technology leader is only mentioned in passing" (Creighton, 2003, p. 3). The digital portfolio can serve as a powerful tool for faculty to infuse technology systematically into the curriculum.

School leader candidates also benefit from developing digital portfolios. General benefits of the portfolio process apply to both teacher candidates and to school leader candidates. These include: self-assessment and reflection, personal satisfaction and renewal, empowerment, collaboration, and holistic assessment.

In addition, specific benefits have been identified for school leader candidates. For example, Yerkes and Guaglianone note that "often begun as part of graduate coursework, the administrative portfolio may be used to self-evaluate, monitor professional growth and development, document specific competencies, or prepare for a job interview" (1998, p. 28). Also, including the standards-based digital portfolio in the educational leadership curriculum prepares school leader candidates to model and use both portfolio assessment and technology when they become school leaders. These benefits are crucial as "aspiring principals must become proficient in developing and applying technology skills, such as designing Web pages and electronic portfolios, and participating in video conferencing" (Chirichello, 2001, p. 47).

Finally, in addition to developing proficiency with a complex array of hardware and software applications, the portfolio process addresses critical needs among many practitioners. As noted by Kilbane and Milman, "two knowledge areas in which many principals require development are technology and authentic assessment. The creation of a portfolio in digital format provides principals a much-needed venue for developing knowledge and skills in these areas" (2003, p. 147).

In using technology, school leaders must become activists. "Education administrators must envision, facilitate, model and embrace technology" (Metropolitan Planning Council, 2002, p. 22). In particular, "there is a dynamic shift occurring in this country as we move from traditional definitions of learning and course design to models of engaged learning that involve more student interaction, more connections among students, more involvement of teachers as facilitators, and more emphasis on technology as a tool for learning" (Jones, Valdez, Nowakowski, & Rasmussen, 1999, p. 2).

With regard to knowledge of authentic assessment, portfolio use by school leaders facilitates leadership effectiveness, enhances student achievement, enhances the professional development of teachers, and facilitates collaboration and communication (Marcoux, Brown, Irby,

& Lara-Alecio, 2003). Another study found portfolios useful to school leaders "as evidence of improvement; as organizer, as record of achievement; as collection of work samples" (Wildy & Wallace, 1998, p. 126). Thus, just as the use of the digital portfolio process benefits educational leadership faculty and school leader candidates, it is also a tool for using technology and authentic assessment while providing personal and professional benefits to school leaders in the field.

However, there are challenges associated with the use of standards-based digital portfolios. Given the paucity of research on digital portfolios, some of these challenges are extrapolated from the more general literature on the portfolio process. In general, there are five major challenges associated with the development of digital portfolios.

First, using digital portfolios in the curriculum requires extensive and careful planning. Second, creating a portfolio is labor-intensive. A third challenge is that it is time-consuming. Fourth, evaluating the portfolio is complicated by the variety of possible artifacts; "the more diverse the documentation, the more difficult it becomes to compare and evaluate the portfolio (Constantino & De Lorenzo, 2002, p. 7)." Fifth, the complex and changing nature of hardware and software requires additional commitment of human and capital resources.

In addition to these more general challenges cited in the literature, Wildy and Wallace conducted a study of school leaders and their use of the portfolio process for the purpose of accountability and identified tensions or challenges "between theory and practice; between public and private demands of portfolios; between the practical nature of leaders' work and the reflective nature of the portfolio; between the portfolio as product and as process; [and] between choice and compliance" (1998, p. 123).

There is no one set of strategies appropriate for addressing all of these challenges in every educational setting. Connecting theory and practice, while not the result of using a digital portfolio, can occur when a digital portfolio is required. Because the digital portfolio is much more easily shared with colleagues, it lends itself to collaboration.

At the same time, however, reflection is a personal endeavor. Thus, there is a tension between the public nature of a digital portfolio and the private reflection of the creator. With regard to the tension, Wildy and Wallace found that "the inquiring, self-critical, analytical and reflective processes of a portfolio culture are also at odds with the school expectations of leaders to be decisive, confident and authoritative" (1998, p. 11).

Whether a digital portfolio is a product, a process, or both is a challenge that educational leadership faculty and school leader candidates will need to explore carefully. The interesting tension between choice and compliance speaks directly to the development of this book. Educational leadership faculty should carefully consider how many guidelines they provide for constructing a digital portfolio and how much choice they give school leader candidates in the structure and content of the digital portfolio.

Clearly we recommend a balance between these two. At the same time, establishing clear hardware and software standards will ease access and may reduce the amount of training needed. Typically, educational leadership faculty using portfolios generally provide an outline for the content of the digital portfolio.

The following strategies will help meet these challenges. First, provide sufficient time, technology training, and other resources to faculty in order to develop the strategies and tools necessary to incorporate the digital portfolio into the curriculum. Second, pilot the standards-based digital portfolio process in one or more courses and expand to the entire curriculum over time. Third, provide templates and tools for school leader candidates to choose from in developing digital portfolios. Fourth, provide partially completed examples of digital portfolios to stimulate student creativity. Fifth, provide ample computer laboratory time. Sixth, use lower level technology software and hardware initially, and incorporate increasingly more sophisticated technology as training and skill level warrant.

CONCLUSION

This text is designed as a handbook that can be adapted for use by educational leadership faculty, school leader candidates, and school leaders for a variety of uses. It can be used as a primary or supplemental text in the educational leadership curriculum or for staff development training. The three different templates, one in TaskStream, one in LiveText, and

INTRODUCTION   xix

one in PowerPoint, are consistent with our view that there is no single "best way" to develop a standards-based digital school leader portfolio.

Resources for using this text are available at http://tiny.cc/Digital_Portfolio. If you launch the WFS Web View, simply ignore the login on the left side of the page. The Digital Portfolio Resources on the site include instructions for accessing LiveText, instructions for accessing TaskStream, and resources for PowerPoint portfolios, including a template. Those using TaskStream or LiveText will find resources on those sites when they open their accounts. Note also that many of the documents were composed in Word 2007. If you have an older version of Word and have difficulty opening those documents (their extension is *.docx*), you will need to download the Office File Converter from Pack http://office.microsoft.com.

This book is organized as follows:

Chapter 1 provides an introduction to the implication of technology on schooling and school leaders.

Chapter 2 provides a brief history of the development and use of standards-based digital portfolios.

Chapter 3 details a suggested outline and design of the digital portfolio.

Chapter 4 provides an overview of various digital options and criteria for selecting from among these options.

Chapter 5 details a suggested outline and design of the digital portfolio using PowerPoint.

Chapter 6 details a suggested outline and design of the digital portfolio using TaskStream.

Chapter 7 details a suggested outline and design of the digital portfolio using LiveText.

Chapter 8 addresses the presentation or evaluation of the standards-based digital portfolio.

A list of references is included at the end of the text.

TECHNOLOGY AND SCHOOL LEADERS

It is arguable that in the last two decades of the twentieth century, nothing has influenced the U.S. educational enterprise more than technology. In fact, by 2005, the pervasive use of technology in U.S. schools included "an exponentially growing number of software and hardware applications for learning and instruction, school operations, management, and security systems" (Lackney, 2005, p. 522). In the few years since then, all aspects of education have been affected by technology in general, and computers, in particular.

This phenomenon, the pervasive influence of technology in schools, requires that school leaders be particularly knowledgeable and aware of how technology affects schools and how it can be used, particularly in four broad areas: communication, the instructional program, school infrastructure, and school management.

COMMUNICATION

One of the most fascinating trends associated with the influx of technology in U.S. society in general, and in elementary and secondary education in particular, is how it has changed social and cultural norms and expectations regarding communication. *How, when, what,* and *with whom* we communicate have all been profoundly changed due to technology. These changes, too numerous to itemize, can be illustrated with a few examples.

How we communicate has been transformed by our use of technology. We still talk in person, and we still use POTS (plain old telephone service), but we also use e-mail, voicemail, text messaging, video calls, blogs, and video and voice streaming. What these tools portend for the future is hard to imagine. Among teenagers, "[t]here has been explosive growth in creative and authoring activities by students on social networking sites in recent years" (National School Boards Association, 2007, p. 1). Of students with online access, 96% report that they have used one or more social networking technologies. Their activities include sharing music, sharing videos, sharing photos, site-building, blogging, and creating content.

Verbal communication is becoming briefer: an e-mail is usually brief and pointed, halfway between conversation and a letter; a text message exchange is the equivalent of a written conversation; a tweet (used on Twitter.com) is limited to 140 characters (less than two typed lines). As a result, Internet slang has entered the lexicon (e.g., IMHO, "in my humble opinion," and LOL, "laughing out loud"), some written communication has become nonverbal (e.g., emoticons such as :-) to indicate pleasure or ;-) for a wink), and using all caps is the equivalent of YELLING OR SCREAMING.

What we communicate is also changing in interesting and important ways. Of particular relevance to school leaders and teachers is the fact that students are increasingly using technology to communicate in relation to educational issues. In fact, 59% of online students say they talk about education-related topics, including college or college planning; learning outside of school; news; careers or jobs; politics, ideas, religion or morals; and schoolwork" (National School Boards Association, 2007). Moreover, 50% of online students say they talk specifically about schoolwork.

When we communicate has become "practically always" and is a shift from the cultural norm of reserving communication to designated times and places. As a result of new communication norms and the new tools noted above, people are expected to respond to various forms of digital communication much more quickly than was previously the case. For example, a response to a text message or a tweet is expected almost immediately. Similarly, an e-mail is usually answered within hours of when it was sent, whereas sending and receiving a response to a letter takes days.

Who we communicate with has expanded dramatically as a result of technology. Students and teachers alike communicate on social networks like Facebook and MySpace, broadcast video on YouTube, and share photos on a number of sites. In addition, teachers share ideas and insights through online special interest groups (SIGs) in professional associations, in newsgroups associated with teaching or other interests, and by writing or commenting on blogs.

One of the newer forums for communication is the multiuser virtual environment (MUVE), or virtual world. MUVEs allow users not only to talk and share resources, but to work with each other using personalized animated characters, or "avatars," which travel around the three-dimensional virtual worlds. Some of these virtual worlds, like Whyville, Harvard's River City Project, and Indiana University's Quest Atlantis, are designed for learning, while others like Second Life and Teen Second Life are more general (though both have a strong education presence in their virtual worlds).

Despite this ability to expand communication, technology also has the confounding capacity to isolate people from interaction with others. Much has been written about computer games and the Internet and their capacity to create virtual interaction for people in lieu of personal contact with others, but communicating through an avatar is not the same as personal contact. Even distance learning, designed for digitized communication as it is, limits personal contact.

The implications for teaching and learning associated with students having dual forms of "reality," one digitized and one grounded in the physical world, has only just recently begun to be investigated. Not surprisingly, students and young adults are in the vanguard of social networking through the creation of Web pages, blogs, social networking sites like Facebook, and communication sites like Twitter. In the future, teachers, parents, and school leaders will also be influenced by the opportunities for expanding the range of those with whom they communicate.

How communication among the world citizenry will change cultural norms and values here and abroad is a source of speculation as it affects society in general and schooling in particular. However, it is clear that the pattern of present and anticipated use of technology, both as a medium of instruction and as a content area in teacher candidate preparation programs, will increase teachers' expectations that school leaders provide resources and support for using technology in the instructional program.

INSTRUCTIONAL PROGRAM

Delivery of the instructional program is rapidly changing due to technology. Perhaps the most dramatic change in curriculum delivery is the growth of distance learning in Pre–12 schools. Data related to distance learning reveal startling growth in the use of technology in the delivery of the instructional program. "During the 12-month 2004–05 school year, 37 percent of public school districts and 10 percent of all public schools nationwide had students enrolled in technology-based distance education courses. These percentages represent an estimated 5,670 school districts and 9,050 public schools in the country" (Zandberg & Lewis, 2008, p. 63). In these schools, 86% of students accessed their online courses from school.

In the years since these data were gathered, the numbers have inevitably continued to increase. In 2008, the National Center for Educational Statistics (NCES) surveyed 1,600 public school districts regarding technology in the schools; from their 92% response, NCES reported that 66% of elementary districts and 78% of secondary districts offered online curricula to students (Gray & Lewis, 2009, p. 12).

Complementing this rise in distance education is the increased use of technology in ordinary classrooms. In regular classrooms, many teachers have moved well beyond drill and practice software and are using technology to develop higher order thinking skills at all grade levels.

Teaching tools include graphic organizers like *Kidspiration* and *Inspiration*; instant messaging to share students' thoughts; class Web pages complete with calendars, assignments, activities, and links to resources;

digital stories and blogs; wikis (collaboratively written Web sites) to teach writing, biology, or any other subject; geospatial technologies such as Google Earth and Virtual Earth in geography classes; math software like *Geometer's Sketchpad* or *Cabri*; simulation modules in various subjects, either online or on CD. In special education classrooms, teachers often have specialized technology such as screen readers or adapted keyboards for students with cognitive or motor limitations and advanced online games like *Bloxorz* teach geometry and spatial relations.

These changes in delivery of the instructional program are due in part to the alteration of teacher education preparation programs in two different but complementary ways. Technology is not only a content area of teacher education but it is also used extensively as a method of instruction. A national survey of nearly 1,500 teacher education preparation programs found that virtually all of the programs surveyed incorporated technology as a significant component in the preparation of teacher candidates for initial licensure. "While about half of all of these institutions offered 3- or 4-credit stand-alone courses in educational technology in their programs, many also taught educational technology within methods courses (93%), within the field experiences of teacher candidates (79%), and within content courses (71%)" (Kleiner, Thomas, & Lewis, 2007, p. 17).

As a result of these changes in teacher preparation, teacher education candidates expect to incorporate technology into the curriculum during their field experiences and when they enter the field as practitioners. Of school districts responding to the NCES survey, 83% reported teachers were interested in using technology in classroom instruction.

And yet, while teacher education candidates are being exposed increasingly to technology, both as a method of instruction and as a content area, their experience in the field suggests that schools are often not well prepared to facilitate their use of technology in practice. In fact, a recent study revealed that there are several school-site–based barriers to teacher candidates applying technology-related skills and knowledge during their field experiences, "including competing priorities in the classroom (74%), available technology infrastructure in the schools (73%), and lack of training or skill (64%), time (62%), and willingness (53%) on the part of supervising teachers to integrate technology in their classrooms" (Kleiner et al., 2007, pp. 17–18).

The growing number of teacher candidates with training in technology use and with the assumption that they will be able to use technology in the instructional program, creates greater expectations that school leaders will be knowledgeable in technology and support its use in the school. These expectations will undoubtedly increase in the future.

SCHOOL INFRASTRUCTURE

Technology has not only changed instruction, it has also changed our understanding of the infrastructure of elementary and secondary schools and is having a significant effect on school leadership in the United States. The infrastructure associated with technology includes hardware, software, and school environmental considerations. As one example of the impact of technology on infrastructure, the current mode of delivery for distance learning courses provides a useful illustration of how the combination of hardware and software is altering the mode of instructional delivery. A survey conducted in 2005, investigating the use of technology in distance learning courses in elementary and secondary public schools, revealed that:

> asynchronous Internet technology was used by the greatest percentage of districts with technology-based distance education (58%), . . . two-way interactive video was used as a primary mode of instructional delivery by 47% of districts, . . . synchronous Internet technologies were reported by 24% of districts with technology based distance education, and one-way prerecorded video was reported by 11% of districts. (Zandberg & Lewis, 2008, p. 65)

All of these deliveries relied on the Internet. It is a stunning development to note that in a span of less than ten years, virtually all public elementary and secondary school classrooms in the United States were connected to the Internet: "in 2005, 94 percent of public school instructional rooms [classrooms] had Internet access, compared with 3 percent in 1994" (Wells & Lewis, 2006, p. 4). Not only has access to the Internet grown dramatically during this time, but the nature of that access has changed as well. "In 2005, 97 percent of public schools with Internet access used broadband connections to access the Internet . . . [whereas] in 1996, dial-up Internet connections (a type of narrowband connection) were used by about three-fourths (74%) of public schools having Internet access" (Wells & Lewis, 2006, p. 5).

Having expanded the concept of "infrastructure," technology is also changing our understanding of what constitutes a "school." Historically, a school was understood to include the physical plant and grounds. For the most part, the school "infrastructure" meant "bricks and mortar" and other tangible physical assets. Within the confines of a fixed physical space, it was understood that teaching and learning occurred. The infrastructure of today's school, thanks to technological developments, increasingly extends beyond the physical school building. Bricks and mortar still stand, but the technology of the infrastructure allows students to roam far from the building and allows teachers to bring into the building a wealth of material never before imagined.

As schools have improved their Internet access, they have also changed how students and teachers access the Internet. Schools today rely less on desktop computers and more on smaller machines. "In 2005, 19% of public schools provided hand-held computers to students or teachers for instructional purposes, an increase from 10% in 2003" (Wells & Lewis, 2006, p. 7). Schools have also begun purchasing more laptop computers. In 2002, the Maine Learning Technology Initiative was created to provide laptops, software, and wireless networking to elementary and middle schools; in 2009, a consortium of high schools extended that initiative by purchasing 3,000 netbook computers. These smaller, less powerful computers are ideal for Internet use and designed to use Web-based applications (e.g., spreadsheets, graphics programs). Some schools see the netbook as a first step to moving from print materials to digital materials.

Within schools, wireless access has become more common because the cost of wireless connections is now competitive with wired access. A rapidly emerging trend is the growth in schools using wireless Internet connections. The growth of wireless connectivity is evidenced by the fact that "forty-five percent of public schools with Internet access used wireless connections in 2005, an increase from 32 percent in 2003" (Wells & Lewis, 2006, p. 5).

As all these developments suggest, a school's infrastructure now includes its Internet connection, its wired and wireless access points, the devices dedicated to student use, and the software and networks that allow the interaction of everything and everyone.

SCHOOL MANAGEMENT

Finally, technology is dramatically changing the management of schools and how school leaders function. Management of the school relative to technology includes such diverse issues as strategic planning, implementation, and evaluation; security; data storage, retrieval, and use; professional development; and funding. With the exponential growth in the access and use of technology in the schools, it is essential that school leaders assume responsibility for the development of a comprehensive technology strategic plan.

Planning

As a part of the planning process, school leaders need to assess continually the efficiency and effectiveness of the use of technology in schools. "Making an audit of learning technology needs, knowing the status of the [school and] school district's technology infrastructure, and assessing how effectively technology serves school learning, instruction and operations are critical first steps in strategic long-term planning" (Lackney, 2005, p. 524). The strategic planning process should include qualitative and quantitative measures for both formative and summative assessment.

Planning now includes security issues associated with technology use in schools. In order to ensure that students cannot access inappropriate material on the Internet, "under the Children's Internet Protection Act (CIPA), no school may receive E-rate discounts unless it certifies that it is enforcing a policy of internet safety that includes the use of filtering or blocking technology" (Wells & Lewis, 2006, p. 8). By 2005, nearly all schools reported having Internet safety policies as well as using filtering or blocking software.

Decision Making

For management purposes, school leaders increasingly rely on technology for data-driven decision making. In fact, as of 2005, "89% of public schools indicated they use the Internet to provide data to inform instructional planning at the school level, [and] 87% of public schools reported using the Internet to provide assessment results and data for teachers to use to individualize instruction" (Wells & Lewis, 2006, p. 10).

In recognition of the essential role of professional development in the successful application of technology to achieve various learning and student achievement objectives, "83% of public schools with Internet access indicated that their school or school district had offered professional development to teachers in their school on how to integrate the use of the Internet into the curriculum the 12 months prior to the survey" (Wells & Lewis, 2006, p. 10).

Funding

Funding technology is currently a complex issue for school leaders.

Successful schools have been able to use a wide range of strategies for funding technology outside of the conventional capital and operational budgets by considering charging for services, contacting local outside agencies for seed grant startups, campaigning in the community to raise funds, partnering with other organizations to share costs, soliciting in-kind contributions from private industry for training or equipment, reducing costs through volunteers, marketing a training program or manual designed by the district, and taking full advantage of state and federal [as well as private foundation] funding programs. (Lackney, 2005, p. 523)

Leading by Example

A growing body of literature documents the contemporary use of technology by school leaders and schools. One study that investigated school leaders in Michigan and their use of technology revealed extensive use of hand-held devices for a variety of purposes including "accessing the profiles of students they meet in the hall, . . . accessing budgetary and student achievement data during planning meetings and discussions with teachers, parents, and other administrators, . . . accessing student, parent, and teacher contact information on the fly, . . . keeping a running record of classroom observations for each teacher in a building, . . . [and] using the handheld's camera to document evidence of incidents" (McNabb, 2006, p. 26).

Another study described a Canadian project, the Galileo Educational Network, as a "successful model for technology integration and engaged learning [in which] leaders and teachers at all levels of the school jurisdiction are involved in developing and supporting technology-enabled learning environments for children" (Flanagan & Jacobsen, 2003, p. 129). These studies demonstrate the exemplary use of technology by contemporary school leaders and indicate the potential of technology for a host of present and yet to be imagined management functions.

Regulation

For school leaders, student use of personal interconnected technology has another side: regulation of student use. By 2008, school districts reported having "written policies on acceptable student use of email (84 percent), social networking websites (76 percent), wikis and/or blogs (52 percent), and other Internet use (92 percent)" (Gray & Lewis, 2009, p. 3) as well as cell phones (88%) and iPods/MP3 players (72%). All this regulation indicates just how technologically aware students are, and by extension, how technologically aware school leaders must become.

A new concern in schools is the rise in "sexting," the practice of sending a sexually explicit message or photo of yourself to another. These messages often go viral, spreading throughout a school and community. The Pew Research Center estimates that "8% of 17-year-olds with cell phones have sent a sexually provocative image by text and 30% have received a nude or nearly nude image on their phone" (Lenhart, 2009, p. 2). The spread of such a message can have devastating effects on a young person, as the suicides of an 18-year-old and a 13-year-old in 2009 evidence.

LOOKING TO THE FUTURE

Although it is impossible to predict with any degree of certainty how technology will impact schools and school leaders in the United States in the future, one means for looking into the future is to look at current technology trends. Some of the trends that are already in evidence include: the increased portability of technology, the growth of distributed educational environments, the changing role of school leaders, and changes in cultural norms and expectations.

Portability

Just as the desktop computer of the 1990s shrunk to a laptop, the laptop has morphed into a hand-held device. Children's electronic game machines such as the Nintendo DS are about the size of a 3-by-5 index card, one-inch thick, and not only include gaming and impressive graphics but also a wireless Internet connection, which allows children to play games with others across the country or across the world. High school students carry cell phones with Internet connections that provide not only text messaging but also a connection to popular sites like YouTube and Facebook.

For adults, the computer has shrunk to the size of a cell phone, and smartphones from Apple, BlackBerry, and Nokia not only allow thumb-typing e-mails and text messages but also offer numerous third-party applications. Not only is the computer shrinking, but it is less reliant on wires, including wires for speakers or for synchronizing with other machines.

These trends portend a future in which students will be able to carry with them, anywhere they go, the essential technology tools that they need both for communication and for learning, and as a result, schools will rely less on fixed, single-purpose computer laboratories. Soon schools will be working with this new technology just at they worked with desktop computers and personal digital assistants.

Distributed Learning Environments

These technology trends are dramatically changing the lives of students and, just as significantly, are changing the role and function of teachers and administrators. In the future, the typical school will potentially be the center or the hub of a distributed learning organization. "Learning activities can be liberated from the self-contained classroom, which may become more of a home base to collectively plan learning activities that will take place all over the school site and community" (Lackney, 2005, p. 529).

The convergence of current technologies, including the Internet, telephone, text messaging, facsimile, and the advent of readily available and inexpensive hand-held computing devices is already changing our understanding of what a school is and where schooling takes place. Due to the advent of information technology and telecommunications, the school as an organization will become more physically and temporally distributed across the community in libraries, businesses, community centers, and home in addition to the traditional schoolhouse. Similarly, technology will redefine the role of the teacher and the instructional program:

> Schools that incorporate the technology of the future can offer the best combination of traditional face-to-face instruction—role modeling, socialization, and morale building—and projected benefits of learning with new technologies: increased participation in systems of distributed learning that engage broader communities, learning enhancing representations of concepts and data, a restructuring of teaching and learning roles, and more meaningful assessment practices. (Means, 2001, p. 61)

Role of School Leaders

With the anticipated increase in technology use, school leaders will need to change dramatically their role and function in order to provide the required leadership in this rapidly changing environment. Gosmire and Grady point out that in contemporary U.S. society, "few principals claim to be technology experts" and that "the key to success on the journey is not to know everything, but to ask the right questions" (2007, p. 17). They then offer the following ten questions to help guide principals in their role as technology leaders.

1. What are the technology trends I need to know about?
2. What does the research say about schools and technology?
3. What do I need to know about technology to move my school forward?
4. Are there guidelines to help me?
5. How do I construct a safety net for technology in the school?
6. How do I know I have created effective policies and plans?
7. How do I promote the integration of technology in the classroom?

8. How much will all of this cost and where do I get the funds?
9. How do I work with technology experts?
10. How will I measure success? (Gosmire & Grady, 2007, pp. 17–20)

Cultural Norms and Expectations

In light of these trends, the future will not necessarily ensure the desired impacts on the instructional program, student achievement, or other organizationally prized outcomes. In fact, "at present, technology is often applied in situations that support traditional styles of instruction, such as lecturing with presentation software, rather than using the full potential of technology-enabled instruction to support innovative learning strategies such as self-directed learning and project-based learning" (Lackney, 2005, p. 522).

Based on the examples of the use of technology in teacher preparation programs and the use of technology by P–12 students, it is interesting to observe that both teachers and students tend to lead rather than follow school leaders in the use of technology. Teachers and teacher candidates are better prepared and expect to use technology in the classroom, and yet research indicates that schools and school environments are not as supportive in this regard as teachers would like.

Students are, on average, using more variations of technology and in more innovative ways than school leaders. In fact, "non-conformists—students who step outside of online safety and behavior rules—are on the cutting edge of social networking, with online behaviors and skills that indicate leadership among their peers" (National School Boards Association, 2007, p. 2). And who are these nonconformists?

> About one in five (22 percent) of all students surveyed, and about one in three teens (31 percent), are nonconformists, students who report breaking one or more online safety or behavior rules, such as using inappropriate language, posting inappropriate pictures, sharing personal information with strangers or pretending to be someone they are not. (National School Boards Association, 2007, pp. 2–3)

These nonconformist students, while gifted with "an extraordinary set of traditional and 21st century skills" are at the same time "significantly more likely than other students to have lower grades, which they report as a mix of Bs and Cs, or lower than other students" (National School Boards Association, 2007, p. 4).

Since school leaders bear a primary role in the creation and development of the school environment, it is fair to question the extent to which they are following and not leading by example in the use of technology in schools. In the future, school leaders will need to become more proactive and less reactive in providing technology leadership in elementary and secondary schools in America. We hope that creating a digital portfolio will be a step toward providing that leadership.

Excerpts from this chapter are taken with permission from: Hauser, G. M., & Koutouzos, D. W. (2009). Technology training and professional development of school leaders in the U.S.A.: The critical need for reform. In Saleh, I. M., & Khine, M. S. (Eds.), *Transformational leadership and educational excellence: Learning organizations in the Information Age* (pp. 245–265). Rotterdam: Sense Publishers B.V.

2

HISTORY OF THE STANDARDS-BASED DIGITAL SCHOOL LEADER PORTFOLIO

This chapter explores essential questions related to digital school leadership portfolios: What is a standards-based digital portfolio? Who uses them? How are they used? Why are they used? It also offers background on the characteristics, purposes, uses, and audiences for a standards-based digital portfolio. We begin by discussing how the school leader or candidate can individualize the digital school leader portfolio to accommodate his or her professional interests and needs.

WHAT IS A STANDARDS-BASED DIGITAL PORTFOLIO?

The term *standards-based digital portfolio* is a complicated concept best understood by examining its parts. The qualifiers "digital" and "standards-based" help place "portfolio" in context.

Portfolios

We shall begin by exploring the term *portfolio*. It might be surprising to know just how widely portfolios are used today. Although portfolios were initially used mainly in the visual arts, they have more recently been adapted to a host of diverse academic disciplines from medicine to library science. Interest in portfolios in modern U.S. society is evident by their use at the local, state, national, and international levels.

Since the early 1990s, there has been a growing body of literature on using portfolios in teacher education, counselor education, and school leadership. Portfolios have only been widely used in higher education, particularly in schools, colleges, and departments of education, since the 1990s. Educational professionals began using portfolios because of the concept of authentic assessment (Wiggins, 1989).

Authentic assessment is sometimes termed as authentic intellectual achievement, which has three characteristics, namely, "construction of knowledge, disciplined inquiry, and value beyond school" (Newmann, Marks, & Gamoran, 1996, p. 282). Constructing knowledge requires production rather than a restatement of information. Disciplined inquiry integrates prior knowledge, develops an in-depth understanding of a problem or relationship, and requires elaborate communication of findings. The third criterion, value beyond school, means applying learning to life experiences. Assessment refers to learning theory and practice beyond the narrow traditional forms of psychological testing and measurement.

A portfolio, in the context of this book, is an authentic assessment tool used by school leaders and school leader candidates to demonstrate intellectual accomplishment. "The portfolio not only offers a tool for authentic assessment but also a means for students to be reflective practitioners, emphasizing the how and why as much as the what" (Lombardi, 2008, p. 10).

Standards

As a tool to document intellectual accomplishment, the portfolio is substantively guided by professional standards, thus the qualifier "standards-based." This emphasis on standards in particular, and testing and measurement in general, is an outgrowth of the wave of school reform that began with the publication of *A Nation at Risk: The Imperative for Educational Reform* (National Commission for Excellence in Education, 1983).

Since the early 1990s, state and national standards and their purported objective outcomes have been viewed as the principal means to assess student achievement, teacher competence, and school leader quality. In regard to school leadership, "implementing the No Child Left Behind Act (NCLB) of 2001 is forcing us to confront the weaknesses of contemporary school leadership and is making it impossible to ignore the escalating need for higher quality principals—individuals who have been prepared to provide the instructional leadership necessary to improve student achievement" (Hale & Moorman, 2003, p. 1). The portfolio shows promise as a way for school leaders to respond to these trends.

One of the most important events for national professional standards occurred in 1994 when the National Policy Board for Educational Administration (NPBEA) formed the Interstate School Leader Licensure Consortium (ISLLC) to develop school leader standards (Murphy, 2003). The NPBEA is an association of ten organizations interested in school leadership, which includes the National Council for the Accreditation of Teachers (NCATE), the University Council for Educational Administration (UCEA), the American Association of Colleges of Teacher Education (AACTE), and others. As created by the NPBEA, the ISLLC included twenty-four member states as well as other organizations interested in school leadership. At the time the standards were developed, the NPBEA also created the Educational Leadership Constituency Council (ELCC) to oversee national recognition of programs based on those standards (National Policy Board for Educational Administration, 2002).

The six ISLLC Standards, published in 1996 and revised in 2008, identify an education leader as one who promotes the success of every student by:

1. facilitating the development, articulation, implementation, and stewardship of a vision of learning that is shared and supported by all stakeholders;
2. advocating, nurturing, and sustaining a school culture and instructional program conducive to student learning and staff professional growth;
3. ensuring management of the organization, operation, and resources for a safe, efficient, and effective learning environment;
4. collaborating with faculty and community members, responding to diverse community interests and needs, and mobilizing community resources;

5. acting with integrity, fairness, and in an ethical manner;
6. understanding, responding to, and influencing the larger political, social, economic, legal, and cultural context. (Council of Chief State School Officers, 2008)

In the revised 2008 ISLLC Standards, each standard is followed by three to nine functions—actions that move school leaders toward achieving the standard. In contrast, the 1996 standards included three dimensions or elements to each standard: knowledge, dispositions, and performances.

Another important set of standards for school leaders, developed by the Technology Standards for School Administrators (TSSA) Collaborative, were published in 2001 (TSSA Collaborative, 2001). The TSSA Collaborative included leading national and international school leadership and technology associations such as the American Association of School Administrators (AASA), the National School Boards Association (NSBA), the National Association of Elementary School Principals (NAESP), the National Association of Secondary School Principals (NASSP), the Association of Education Service Agencies (AESA), and the International Society for Technology in Education (ISTE), among others. The primary goal of the Collaborative was to develop national standards for what school administrators "should know and be able to do to optimize the effective use of technology" (TSSA Collaborative, 2001).

These standards complemented the work done by ISTE in developing its National Technology Standards (NETS) for students and teachers. Building on the work of the TSSA, in 2002, ISTE published its National Technology Standards for Administrators (NETS-A). To keep the standards relevant, ISTE undertook a three-year process to refresh the standards and in June 2009 published its revised NETS-A:

1. Educational Administrators inspire and lead development and implementation of a shared vision for comprehensive integration of technology to promote excellence and support transformation throughout the organization.
2. Educational Administrators create, promote, and sustain a dynamic, digital-age learning culture that provides a rigorous, relevant, and engaging education for all students.

3. Educational Administrators promote an environment of professional learning and innovation that empowers educators to enhance student learning through the infusion of contemporary technologies and digital resources.
4. Educational Administrators provide digital-age leadership and management to continuously improve the organization through the effective use of information and technology resources.
5. Educational Administrators model and facilitate understanding of social, ethical, and legal issues and responsibilities related to an evolving digital culture.

Each standard is supplemented by three to five performance indicators (International Society for Technology in Education, 2009).

The content of the standards-based digital school leader portfolio in this book is guided primarily by the six ISLLC Standards and the five standards of NETS-A. Other sets of criteria, such as local, district, and state standards and academic course or program expectations can be added at the discretion of the school leader or school leader candidate.

Digital

With a better understanding of the term standards-based, we now turn to the qualifier "digital." You have likely read about both digital portfolios and electronic portfolios. Are they the same thing? Experts say they are not. As pointed out by Helen Barrett, "an electronic portfolio contains artifacts that may be in analog form, such as a video tape, or may be in computer-readable form; in a digital portfolio, all artifacts have been transformed into computer-readable form" (2000, p. 14).

Because this book provides a guide to develop portfolios that are completely in computer-readable form, it uses the term digital instead of the more commonly used term electronic. Creating a digital portfolio has the advantages of "affect[ing] student understanding of how a portfolio functions and also improv[ing] students' computer skills," as well as leading to "clearer understanding of the interrelation of standards and the connection of those standards to [students'] own performance" (Hauser, Koutouzos, & Olson, 2005, p. 313).

The early 1990s marked an important milestone for how schools use standards-based digital portfolios as an authentic assessment tool with the Exhibitions Project, an initiative by the Coalition for Essential Schools. "Much more than an electronic file cabinet, digital portfolios are transforming assessment—and becoming a tool for school reform" (Niguidula, 1997, p. 26). As part of the school reform effort, it is imperative that school leaders, trainers, and school leader candidates learn from personal experience how to develop and use standards-based digital portfolios.

WHO USES THEM?

Practitioners in a wide range of disciplines use portfolios to document professional growth and facilitate career advancement. These practitioners include music educators, higher education faculty members, technical writers, and school leaders. Professional trainers use portfolios to evaluate candidate performance in such fields as elementary education, secondary education, school counselor, language and literacy, teacher leadership, and special education.

More recently, portfolios have been used by principals and other leadership professionals, trainers, and candidates. Faculty members in school leadership programs are increasingly requiring portfolio assessments in lieu of comprehensive examinations and to show academic achievement in general. Professional candidates use portfolios to comply with course requirements and advance their careers. In sum, there is growing evidence that educators—including school leaders and school leader candidates—use portfolios.

HOW ARE THEY USED?

There are several different ways to categorize how portfolios are used depending on who uses them. For example, Wolf and Sui-Runyon (1996) identify three types of portfolios: the ownership portfolio, the feedback portfolio, and the accountability portfolio. The ownership portfolio is used to guide self-directed learning. In this instance, the "how" is guided by personal learning objectives and outcomes. In the feedback portfolio, the leader or leader candidate and a peer coach, collaborator, supervisor, or instructor use the portfolio to collaborate on learning goals and outcomes. The feedback portfolio provides feedback to guide pedagogical practice and professional growth. The accountability portfolio is guided primarily by district requirements and professional standards or by an instructor to evaluate student achievement. According to Wolf and Sui-Runyon, these different types of student portfolios can be distinguished based on authorship, audience, structure, content, and process.

There are other alternative classifications of portfolios. Brown and Irby (2001), for example, describe four different types of portfolios. For our purposes, however, three broad uses for portfolios will be considered, namely, evaluative, developmental, and career. The evaluative portfolio provides a summative evaluation of a school leader's performance or school leader candidate's performance related to various criteria. A school leader might develop an evaluative portfolio in cooperation with a supervisor in response to local, district, state, or ISLLC Standards.

There are several other examples of portfolios being used in connection with school leader evaluation (Cruz, 1998; Marcoux, Brown, Irby, & Lara-Alecio, 2003). School leader candidates, working with school leaders, might develop a digital evaluation portfolio to document academic achievement. More specifically, school leader candidates might use digital portfolios to document their achievement of knowledge, performance, and dispositions of the ISLLC Standards through digital artifacts for coursework or practical experiences. A key feature of the evaluation portfolio is that it is evaluated externally.

The developmental portfolio can be used to record professional or academic growth. School leaders might use digital portfolios to document their achievement of performance standards associated with continuing professional development units (CPDUs). School leader candidates might develop a digital portfolio to record personal and professional growth as they complete their academic program. Because it is for personal use and not for evaluative use, it is shared with others at the discretion of the creator.

The career portfolio can be used by school leaders or school leader candidates who are seeking employment or professional advancement. In this case, school leaders have the opportunity to assemble reflections and artifacts to document their accomplishments far beyond the standard cover letter and résumé.

WHY ARE THEY USED?

Barrett (1998, 2000) and Sheingold (1992) identify many advantages in using digital portfolios. Digital portfolios require minimum storage space, in contrast to bulky paper portfolios. This is particularly important for school leaders interested in storing work completed by school leader candidates. It is much easier to create duplicate copies of digital portfolios. Copies are useful for backup and career advancement. Digital portfolios are also more portable than paper portfolios. A digital portfolio stored on a CD or flash drive requires very little space, and the Web-based digital portfolio requires no digital space locally.

Digital portfolios have a very long shelf life in contrast to paper portfolios, which deteriorate over time. One of the caveats to this long shelf life, however, is changes in software and hardware. Diskettes and Zip disk drives, once popular storage mediums, are no longer found on new computers. Consider also some of the difficulties commonly experienced with different versions of Microsoft Office software. The point is that older or obsolete versions of software and hardware can make accessing some artifacts in a digital portfolio difficult. Still, digital portfolios are more accessible than paper portfolios. This is particularly true of the Web-based versions of digital portfolios, accessible through any computer with an Internet connection.

The digital portfolio is a potent way for school leaders and school leader candidates to increase their technology skills and model best practices associated with technology. Digital portfolios can be used to facilitate standards-based, learner-centered learning. Using more than one set of professional standards is particularly easy to accomplish with digital portfolios through Web-based digital portfolio tools. Some Web-based tools allow users to browse through different sets of standards, then choose and interrelate appropriate sets of standards. Kilbane and Milman summarize: "digital portfolios help showcase principals' knowledge, leadership, and technology competence, support teaching portfolio initiatives, and teach principals about themselves and their practice" (2003, p. 143).

DEFINITIONS OF PORTFOLIOS IN THE FIELD OF EDUCATION

Given that portfolios are used as an alternative form of authentic assessment in so many subspecialties in education, it is not surprising that there are numerous definitions of portfolios in the literature. These definitions, while seemingly very different, are useful because we can see in them commonalities.

A portfolio is typically contingent upon who is creating it, for whom, and for what purpose. For example, Arter offered a general definition of the student portfolio as a "purposeful collection of student work that tells the story of the student's efforts, progress and achievement in a given area" (1992, p. 3).

In counselor education programs, potential use of portfolios has been described as follows: "in conjunction with traditional assessment approaches already established, the student counseling portfolio can provide interesting and important documentation for clinical growth and development [and] offer a solution to training problems often encountered by professional counselor programs" (Baltimore, Hickson, George, & Crutchfield, 1996, p. 113). Constantino and De Lorenzo note a wide range of definitions of portfolios in teacher education literature: "in general, the definitions share many common elements. . . . They consistently affirm the idea that portfolio documentation provides authentic evidence of a teacher's work and is a vehicle for fostering reflection on the art and practice of teaching" (2002, p. 2).

Wolf and Siu-Runyon identify the following characteristics common to all portfolios: "no matter the particulars of any portfolio system, all portfolios are constructed for clear and sound purposes, contain diverse collections of . . . work and records of progress assembled over time, are framed by reflections and enriched through collaboration, and have as their ultimate aim the advancement of . . . learning" (1996, p. 3).

THE PORTFOLIO CONCEPTUAL MODEL

How do you make sense of all these differences? One way to understand the *who, what,* and *how* of a portfolio is to consider three dimensions, namely, the constituency, the content, and the purpose. The constituency refers to *who is using the portfolio*, the content refers to *what is contained in the portfolio*, and the purpose refers to *how the portfolio is used*. See Figure 2.1 for a useful graphic representation of these dimensions.

As mentioned previously, digital portfolios, with some editing, can address a combination of constituencies, content, and purposes. The three constituencies under consideration include school leaders, school leader faculty members, and school leader candidates. The content of the portfolio addresses local, state, and national standards. The academic program requirements at a university or the criteria of a school district are local standards. State school leadership standards are state

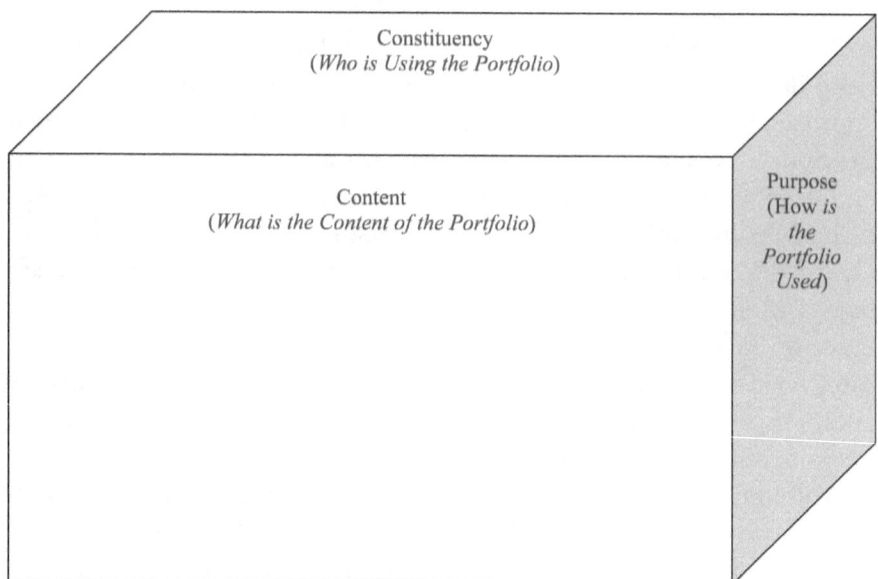

Figure 2.1. Three Dimensions of the Portfolio

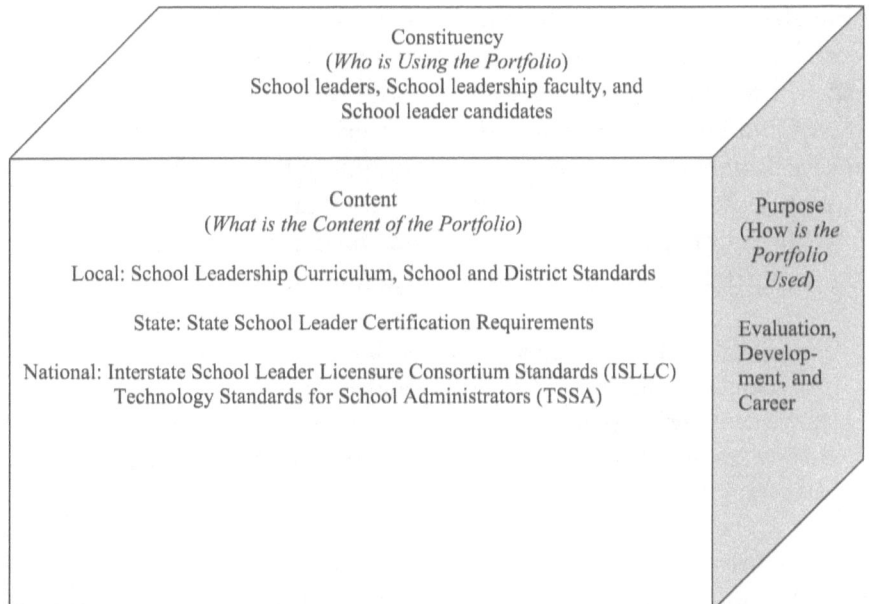

Figure 2.2. Three Dimensions of the Portfolio Related to School Leadership Preparation and Practice

standards, and the ISLLC Standards are national standards. The three purposes for a portfolio are evaluative, developmental, and career. Figure 2.2 shows the possible permutations of constituency, content, and purpose of school leadership digital portfolios.

DEFINITION OF THE STANDARDS-BASED DIGITAL SCHOOL LEADER PORTFOLIO

There are several definitions of the school leader portfolio in the literature. For example, Meadows and Dyal define the portfolio for school leader candidates as follows: "Leadership portfolios allow aspiring administrators to demonstrate through genuine and practical evidence the skills, practices, and strategies essential to becoming successful, competent school leaders" (1999, p. 304).

Brown and Irby offer the following definition: "The principal portfolio, whether for the purposes of professional or academic growth, evaluation, or career advancement, is a collection of thoughtfully selected exhibits or artifacts and reflections indicative of an individual's experiences and ability to lead and of the individual's progress toward and/or attainment of established goals or criteria" (2001, p. 2). Because our focus here is on standards-based content of the portfolio in a digital format, these prior definitions are not sufficient.

With Figure 2.2 as a model for the standards-based school leader digital portfolio, refer to the following definition:

> The digital portfolio is used by school leaders, school leadership faculty members, and school leader candidates (*who*) to document the knowledge, performance, and dispositions required by local, state, and national professional standards (*what*) for evaluative, developmental, and career purposes (*how*).

This inclusive definition, while accommodating the complex differences in constituencies (*who*), content (*what*), and purposes (*how*) as outlined in Figure 2.2, is not discrete enough to meet the diverse interests and needs of individuals.

Several possible definitions are provided below to illustrate the differences in constituency, content, and purpose and the *who*, *what*, and *how*. The following is a sample definition of a digital portfolio used by a school leader for professional development:

> The digital portfolio is used by a school leader (*who*) to document the knowledge, performance, and dispositions required by district and state standards (*what*—local and state) as required for continuing professional development (*how*).

A sample definition of a digital portfolio used by a school leader as a tool for career advancement follows:

> The digital portfolio is used by a school leader (*who*) to document the knowledge, performance, and dispositions required by district and state standards (*what*—local and state) for career advancement (*how*).

And here is a sample definition of a digital portfolio used by a school leader for evaluation:

HISTORY OF THE SCHOOL LEADER PORTFOLIO

The digital portfolio is used by a school leader (*who*) to document the knowledge, performance, and dispositions required by district and state standards (*what*—local and state) for the purposes of evaluation (*how*).

The following is a sample definition of a school leader candidate digital portfolio used for evaluation:

> The digital portfolio is used by a school leader candidate (*who*) to document the knowledge, performance, and dispositions required in the internship course (*what*—local) for the purposes of evaluation (*how*).

And lastly, a sample definition of a school leader candidate digital portfolio used for career advancement follows:

> The digital portfolio is used by a school leader candidate (*who*) to document the knowledge, performance, and dispositions required in the academic program (*what*—local), state (*what*—state), and ISLLC standards (*what*—national) for the purposes of career advancement (*how*).

Before attempting to design a digital portfolio, develop one or more working definitions. Construct working definitions of the standards-based digital portfolio by completing Figure 2.3. Figure 2.3 also provides space

Constituency	Content	Purpose
Example: *The digital portfolio is a tool used by a school leader*	to document the knowledge, performance, and dispositions required by local, state and national standards	for the purpose of evaluation.
The digital portfolio is a tool used by. . .	to document the. . .	for the purpose of. . .
(Optional 2nd definition) The digital portfolio is a tool used by. . .	to document the. . .	for the purpose of. . .

Figure 2.3. Definition of My Standards-Based Digital Portfolio

to construct more than one definition if you are planning to create more than one version of the digital portfolio. For example, school leader candidates might wish to create one version of the standards-based digital portfolio to comply with an academic program. At the same time, some might wish to create another version of the same digital portfolio for employment purposes. The content and design of each portfolio will be different. You may wish to create your own definition and save it to your digital portfolio. You might use the document created for this purpose at http://tiny.cc/Digital_Portfolio, left-click on Digital Portfolio Resources, left-click Supplemental Resources, left-click on Definition of Digital Portfolio. You may also access this document in Supplemental Resources on TaskStream or LiveText.

SUMMARY

Once you have a working definition of a digital portfolio, expand your understanding by engaging in one or more or the following activities for reflection and portfolio planning:

1. Consider the implications of using the standards-based digital portfolio as an authentic assessment tool with colleagues or practitioners.
2. Compare and contrast the individualized portfolio definition with the definition created by other school leader candidates or other school leaders.
3. Create a matrix that identifies how the individualized digital portfolio might compare and contrast with a traditional format.
4. Access online library resources to identify articles, monographs, and other digital documents and to enrich understanding of one or more of the topics from this chapter.
5. Identify a topic from this chapter on which you would like to read further.
6. Identify online resources to aid in developing the standards-based digital portfolio.

DEVELOPMENT OF THE STANDARDS-BASED DIGITAL SCHOOL LEADER PORTFOLIO

In this chapter we review the outline template for a standards-based digital portfolio and consider linear and nonlinear format options. As a tool for portfolio development, ISLLC 2008 and NETS-A 2009 self-assessments are provided on TaskStream, LiveText, and at http://tiny.cc/Digital_Portfolio for those using PowerPoint. Use them to rate perceived importance and skill level for each standard at the outset and to identify priority elements for demonstrating growth. Examples of project-based activities associated with each standard provide working models. The portfolio self-assessment is a working document to facilitate the identification of objectives, activities, and artifacts associated with the selected elements of each standard.

WHAT MIGHT BE INCLUDED IN THE OUTLINE?

A personalized definition of the standards-based digital portfolio should be created prior to developing a portfolio outline. Understanding who is using the portfolio, what the content of the portfolio is, and how it is being used guides the creation of one or more definitions. Review the definitions of the standards-based digital portfolio in Chapter 2. The personalized definition guides the reader in the development of an outline for the portfolio and is an essential element to review and reflect upon throughout the process.

Developing a general outline is the next step in creating a standards-based digital portfolio. This general outline might include the following sections: (1) personal definition of the standards-based digital portfolio, (2) professional goal statement, (3) leadership philosophy, (4) ISLLC 2008 Standards, (5) NETS-A 2009 Standards, and (6) supplemental material.

The second section, the professional goal statement, is an opportunity for school leaders to describe short- and long-term career aspirations. It would be appropriate in this section to include a hyperlink to a current résumé. For the third section, leadership philosophy, school leaders or school leader candidates can articulate their own personal leadership philosophy grounded in theory, research, and best practice. In the fourth and fifth sections, school leaders or school leader candidates specify the objectives, activities, and artifacts associated with the ISLLC 2008 Standards and the NETS-A 2009 Standards.

Lastly, school leaders or school leader candidates can include supplemental resources not appropriate for inclusion in any other section of the portfolio. Supplemental material might include activity time logs, the internship contract, school or district professional development guidelines, reflective journals, and other similar artifacts.

School leaders and school leader candidates should be concerned primarily about two core questions. Does the outline provide the general structure for how I wish to construct the portfolio? Will the outline make sense to the various readers and reviewers who will examine the portfolio? We strongly encourage modifying and adapting the sample outline in response to these two questions.

Should the Portfolio Be Linear or Nonlinear in Format?

Montgomery and Wiley (2004) describe the easiest way to understand the difference between the two formats as follows: "In that most presentation software is treated as a linear program, the most common use of the programs is to move from one slide to the next, in a specific order"

DEVELOPMENT OF THE SCHOOL LEADER PORTFOLIO

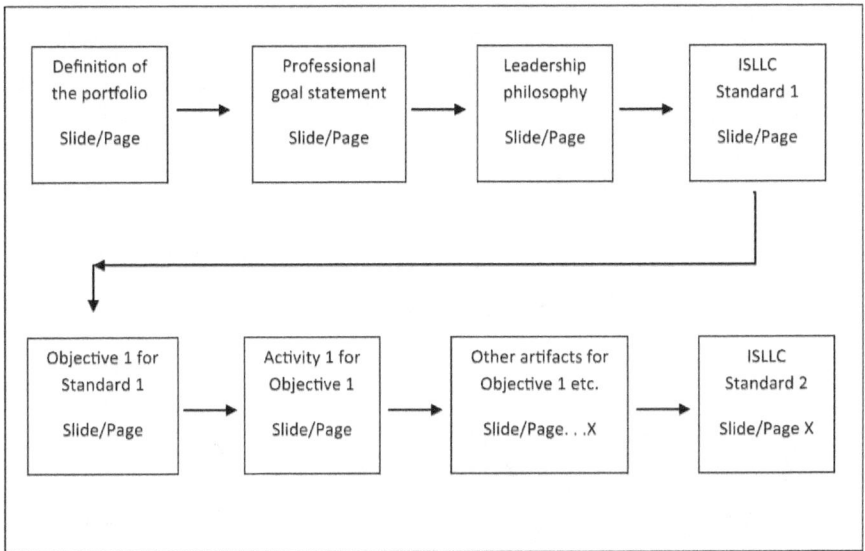

Figure 3.1. Linear Standards-Based Digital Portfolio Outline in PowerPoint, TaskStream, or LiveText

(2004, p. 92). See Figure 3.1. Note that the solid lines display the linear progression from one slide or page to the next.

A nonlinear format "allows the viewer to 'jump' from slide to slide, or slide to a document outside of the presentation software, and then jump back to the original or to a different slide" (Montgomery & Wiley, 2004, p. 93). This technique is called *hyperlinking*. By using this technique, "the author can create hyperlinks either by allowing the viewer to click on the words describing where the hyperlink will go (in a manner similar to most Web page navigation) or by creating a series of 'buttons' that can be 'pushed' by clicking on the button" (Montgomery & Wiley, 2004, p. 93). These hyperlinks allow fluid navigation from slide to slide within the program and to a wide range of artifacts outside of the presentation software. Hyperlinks are typically attached to "buttons," graphics, text, and Web addresses.

Templates for standards-based school leader digital portfolios are available at TaskStream and LiveText and at http://tiny.cc/Digital_Portfolio for those using PowerPoint. These templates are designed by combining features of both the linear and nonlinear format and include examples

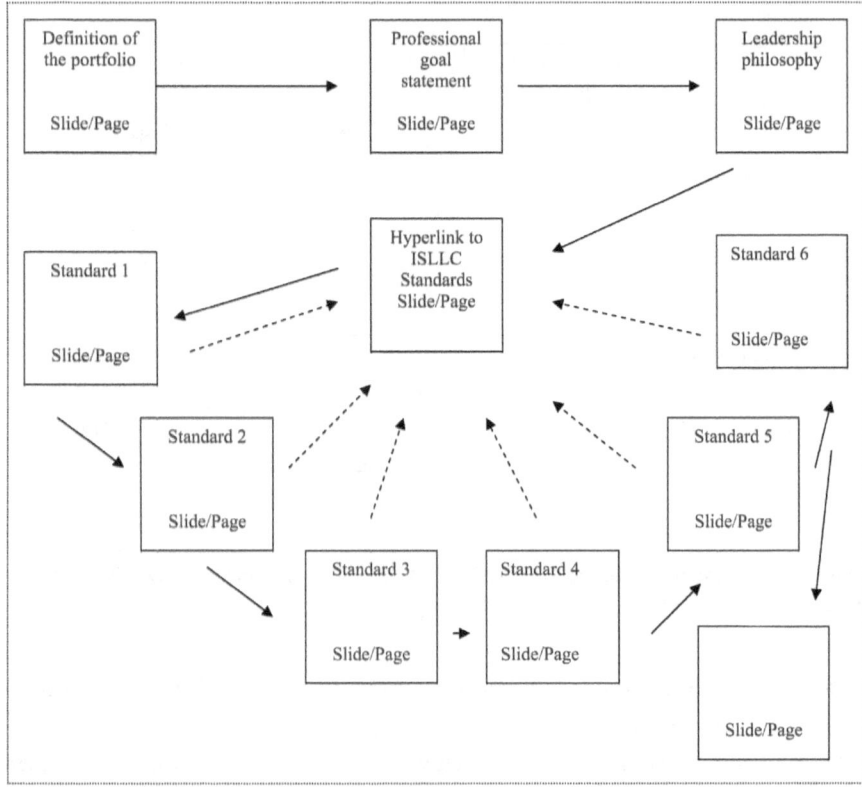

Figure 3.2. Linear and Nonlinear Standards-Based Digital Portfolio Sample Outline

of three different types of hyperlinking. See Figure 3.2 for a sample outline that combines linear and nonlinear features. Note that solid lines display linear progression from slide to slide and dotted lines indicate progression chosen by the viewer.

Activity 1. Consider whether the portfolio should be developed in a linear or nonlinear format. The first few slides or pages in which the school leader or school leader candidate introduces himself or herself to the viewer may make the most sense if they are presented in a linear format. On the other hand, formatting the standards section in a linear format may confuse or, worse, bore the viewer. Therefore, we recommend using a combination of linear and nonlinear format options in the digital portfolio.

Because it is difficult to provide guidelines as to what extent a portfolio should be linear versus nonlinear, it is advisable to have one or more critical friends navigate the portfolio. Critical friends can provide valuable feedback associated with these issues. The original format might change during the development of the digital portfolio. Consider the following questions:

1. To what extent should the portfolio be linear versus nonlinear?
2. What digital portfolio content makes the most sense in a linear format?
3. What digital portfolio content makes the most sense to present in a nonlinear format?

Complete the ISLLC 2008 and the NETS-A 2009 self-assessments related to perceived importance and beginning skill level for each standard and identify priority areas.

The section that contains the professional standards is the most important and complex section of the portfolio. Reflective self-assessment and careful planning are essential in the development of this section. To assist school leaders and school leader candidates with these processes, four instruments that are useful in the planning phase of the digital portfolio are included on TaskStream and LiveText and at http://tiny.cc/Digital_Portfolio for those using PowerPoint. These instruments are: the ISLLC 2008 self-assessment, the NETS-A 2009 self-assessment, the ISLLC 2008 Standards Examples and Worksheets, and the NETS-A 2009 Standards Examples and Worksheets.

The ISLLC 2008 self-assessment includes three scales. In the first scale, you rank the relative importance of each element of each standard. In the second scale, you identify your perceived entry skill level. Ranking the relative importance of each element of these standards is important due to the complexity and number of subelements. Not all of these subelements will be perceived as equally important to either school leaders or school leader candidates. Some internal and external factors affecting these perceptions include education, values, and experience, and the school and community environment. Given the complexity of the number and range of subscales and these internal and external factors, portfolios should focus on the criteria of perceived importance and perceived skill level.

These two self-assessments should be completed before beginning the digital portfolio process and will be used differently depending upon the user. For example, school leaders find their reflection on these scales useful in the development of professional development activities. School leader candidates find their reflection on these scales useful in the development of internship experiences. Given the complexity of the ISLLC 2008 Standards, this self-assessment provides focus for the digital portfolio and a rich source of information that is useful for planning and reflection. In Chapter 8, readers are asked to use the third scale to identify their skill level at the end of the digital portfolio project.

Similarly, the NETS-A 2009 technology self-assessment should be completed at the beginning and at the end of the development of the digital portfolio. As in the case of the ISLLC 2008 self-assessment, the NETS-A 2009 self-assessment is used differently by school leaders, school leader candidates, and school leadership faculty. Using the first two scales, you identify the perceived importance of each element and your perceived entry skill of each NETS-A 2009 Standard. Again, in Chapter 8, you use the third scale to identify culminating skill levels at the end of the digital portfolio project.

Activity 2. Complete the perceived importance and the entry skill level scales of the ISLLC 2008 self-assessment and the NETS-A 2009 self-assessment. Compare and contrast the responses to each of these two instruments. After completion of both the ISLLC 2008 and the NETS-A 2009 self-assessment instruments, identify high priority elements of the various standards. High priority is defined as a function of perceived importance and entry level skill level.

School leaders might consider desired competence as a key factor in determining relative importance among the various elements of the standards. Elements of standards that are perceived as being high in importance and low in skill level should be considered high-priority areas to address in developing the digital portfolio. Likewise, elements of standards that are perceived as low in importance and high in skill level may be considered low-priority areas to address in developing the digital portfolio. There is not an exact formula for determining the elements of the standards that you should address, but self-assessment and careful reflection, based on the two criteria mentioned previously, provide focus for the development of the portfolio.

Fortunately there are several excellent resources to guide school leaders and school leader candidates in thinking and reflecting about establishing priorities from these standards. For example, Capasso and Daresh (2001) provide a number of excellent exercises and activities to facilitate readers developing specific projects and activities associated with the various ISLLC Standards. Martin, Wright, and Danzig (2003) offer exercises and activities to facilitate school leader candidates in addressing these professional standards and in planning the school leader internship experience. Hackmann, Schmitt-Oliver, and Tracy (2002) provide an in-depth analysis for school leader interns of each of the ISLLC Standards and an excellent array of suggested activities and projects for each standard.

Activity 3. Save the ISLLC 2008 Examples-Worksheets file and the NETS-A 2009 Examples-Worksheets file to a flash drive or a hard drive. The files are available at http://tiny.cc/Digital_Portfolio under the Supplemental Resources link; those using TaskStream or from LiveText will find the files under Supplemental Resources. Open and save each file under new file names, for example, My ISLLC 2008 Worksheets and My NETS-A 2009 Worksheets.

Once saved, complete the worksheets and hyperlink to a PowerPoint presentation or upload to either TaskStream or LiveText. The examples and worksheets are provided as a visual illustration of how they can be used to address selected elements of the standards in the digital portfolio. Review the example objective, activities, and artifacts for each standard. The examples illustrate the variety and types of objectives, activities, and artifacts that can be included in a digital portfolio. Also, consider the interrelationship among elements within each set of standards as well as the relationship between the two sets of professional standards. School leaders and school leader candidates will hopefully derive new understanding of the interrelationship among these professional standards.

How Important Is Journaling and Reflection?

One of the most important elements of the digital portfolio is the process of journaling, reflection, and feedback. This aspect is important because the consistent use of reflection, journaling, and feedback from a critical friend provides the basis for deeper understanding and enhances both personal and professional growth during the digital portfolio process.

Dewey recognized the importance of reflection as the "active, persistent, and careful consideration of any belief or supposed form of knowledge in the light of the grounds that support it and the further conclusions to which it tends" (1933, p. 9). Valli identified five different types of reflection that could be used by school leaders and school leader candidates: "technical reflection, reflection-in and on-action, deliberative reflection, personalistic reflection, and critical reflection" (1997, p. 5).

Technical reflection relates to both the content of the reflection and the quality of the reflection. In this context, the ISLLC 2008 Standards and the NETS-A 2009 Standards are used to guide this form of reflection. A school leader or school leader candidate might reflect on a specific leadership task in the context of one or more standards or elements of standards.

Reflection-in and on-action was first described by Schon (1983) in relation to professionals and later adapted to teachers; however, this concept can be applied to school leaders and school leader candidates as well. Reflection-in-action is the careful consideration that occurs during the act of leadership. In contrast to technical reflection, which is informed by external standards, research, and best practices, reflection-in-action is informed by the school leader's values and beliefs as well as the culture and context of the school and community.

Reflection-on-action is the careful consideration that occurs after a leadership task has been completed. In this regard the reflection is informed by school leadership training as well as by experience. Technical reflection is concerned with objective external norms, but reflection-in and on-action are concerned more with the unique dimensions associated with leadership in a particular school and community. Both reflection-in and on-action emphasize the craft knowledge associated with the practice of school leadership.

According to Valli (1997), deliberative reflection is informed by a variety of voices and perspectives, including standards, research, experience, other school leaders, and values and beliefs. These different ways of describing school leader practice often lead to conflicting decisional alternatives for school leaders. It is the careful consideration of these options and their underlying sources of information that are at the heart of deliberative reflection.

Personalistic reflection is heavily influenced by the writings associated with the ethic of care (Katz, Noddings, & Strike, 1999; Noddings, 1984). It is also derived from the personal values, beliefs, and background of the school leader. In personalistic reflection, empathy toward members of the school-community as well as the values of compassion, trust, and loyalty are emphasized. In technical reflection, school leaders are more concerned with professional standards and their universal application; however, in personalistic reflection, school leaders are more concerned about the needs of the individual.

Critical reflection is drawn from the writings of critical theorists such as Paulo Freire (1973), Henry Giroux (2001), and others, and is based on the premise that schooling contributes to social injustice and inequality. Through critical reflection, school leaders consider leadership behavior in the context of social activism as a means to address the needs of the disempowered in the school and community.

All five types of reflection might or might not be appropriate, depending upon the leadership activity. There could be instances in which all five types of reflection are useful for thinking about the leadership activity, and there could be other instances in which only one or two are appropriate. Carefully consider these five types of reflection when planning, implementing, assembling, and assessing the standards-based digital portfolio. The journal artifacts attached to the school leader sample portfolio provide examples of each different type of reflection.

BEGIN TO ASSEMBLE THE STANDARDS-BASED DIGITAL PORTFOLIO

Now begin to assemble the standards-based portfolio. You have already completed the following steps in this process:

1. The development of an individualized definition of the standards-based digital portfolio.

2. The review, reflection, and possible modification of the outline template.
3. The completion of the standards self-assessments and the identification of priorities.
4. The review of sample projects for each standard.
5. The development of proposed objectives, activities, and artifacts for each standard.
6. The development of a digital filing system for the digital portfolio. Although there is no right or wrong method of filing, file names should be brief and clear to assist you and others in viewing the digital portfolio. Consider creating a folder for each standard in My Documents on your computer hard drive. Within each folder include all files associated with that standard. Remember that some artifacts can meet more than one standard and may therefore need to be hyperlinked to other standards as well.
7. Linking the digital assembly of objectives, activities, and artifacts to each standard. There are many different ways to do this, but a simple and effective way is to digitally copy and paste the objectives and activities from the worksheets to the appropriate screen or slides.
8. The continuous reflection and modifications of the design, which affects changes based on personal preferences, the technical proficiency of the reader, and reflection and feedback from a critical friend. With regard to this last point, the Formative Evaluation Rubric can be used to evaluate your own work or it can be shared with a critical friend to receive feedback. This rubric can be accessed at the Supplemental Resources link in TaskStream and LiveText, or at http://tiny.cc/Digital_Portfolio for those using PowerPoint. The Formative Evaluation Rubric guides reflective assessment of the portfolio while it is being developed. School leaders and school leader candidates benefit from using this instrument at various stages in the development of the digital portfolio.

SUMMARY

In this chapter we provided an introduction to the digital portfolio template outline and an overview of a linear and nonlinear outline format.

We explored how to alter the outline template with personalized definitions. Upon completion of the ISLLC 2008 and NETS-A 2009 Standards self-assessments, priority elements were identified. Subsequent to a review of example projects associated for each standard, project-based activities were formulated, including objectives, activities, and artifacts. You are now prepared to begin to assemble the standards-based digital portfolio.

Review the completed examples and worksheets with a critical friend and consider the following questions:

1. Are the plans feasible in terms of your time and resources and the time and resources of others involved?
2. Do the objectives, activities, and artifacts address the identified priorities?
3. How will artifacts be labeled, filed, and stored?
4. What issues and concerns do you have? Explore these with a critical friend.

Complete the Formative Evaluation Rubric (see Supplemental Resources at TaskStream or LiveText, or at http://tiny.cc/Digital_Portfolio for those using PowerPoint) at various stages in the development of the digital portfolio. Also have a critical friend complete the formative rubric each time. Compare and contrast your responses with the responses of the critical friend. Identify strengths as well as opportunities for improvement. Develop strategies to address opportunities for improvement.

4

DIGITAL FORMAT OPTIONS

This chapter provides readers with an overview of the technology involved in preparing a digital portfolio. In particular, we discuss computer requirements for producing a digital portfolio, peripheral hardware that might be needed, development software, and storage mediums for saving and distributing portfolios. By the end of this chapter, you will be prepared to select a digital format for your portfolio.

Just as physical portfolios usually include sections, tabs, and artifacts, digital portfolios include virtual equivalents of these elements. One of the advantages of digital portfolios is that they allow viewers to choose the order in which sections are viewed, much like an Internet site. This interaction has the potential to draw in audiences more readily than a physical portfolio does. Another appealing aspect of digital portfolios is that they can include anything that can be stored on a computer: documents, pictures, audio, video, or combinations of these.

Although most artifacts in the digital portfolio are text, a digital format can contain anything that can be digitized, including publications, snapshots, and video. Digital portfolios are presented using software. Once complete, they are stored on a digital medium (Internet, CD, flash drive) that allows easy access for all potential audiences.

WHAT KIND OF COMPUTER DO I NEED?

To develop a digital portfolio, you can use either a PC or a Mac. The more recent the computer and the operating system, the easier the project will be. This book is written based on a Mac running OS X (10.4 or later versions) or a PC running Windows 7. Please note that earlier versions of Windows will also work. Most of the examples—and all of the instructions in Chapters 5, 6, and 7—are based on a PC and Microsoft Office 2007. If using a Mac, adjust these instructions accordingly.

Specifically, we recommend the following PC configuration: Windows XP or Windows 7; 2 GB RAM minimum (4 GB RAM or more will speed and facilitate the process); 160 GB hard drive, particularly if the portfolio process will involve video editing (see below).

WHAT HARDWARE DO I NEED TO PRODUCE A SCHOOL LEADER PORTFOLIO?

The type of artifacts in the portfolio will determine what hardware is required. Following is a list of peripherals that will be of use in preparing different types of artifacts.

Scanners

Artifacts that are not already in digital format may be converted to digital format through the use of a scanner. Scanners convert photos, drawings, papers, news articles—anything that can be photocopied. Scanned pictures can be cropped so that they include only the most significant part of the image. The process for scanning pictures and photos is different from scanning documents, so be sure to read the scanner directions before beginning. Documents can be scanned and converted into word processor text (which will need to be edited to ensure that the scanning software recognized the text properly) or they can be scanned into PDF files, readable on Adobe Acrobat. A PDF file is essentially a picture of a document and is particularly useful for scanning brochures, booklets, or other documents with graphics.

Cameras

Digital still cameras vary considerably, but all offer different resolutions for the pictures they take. The higher resolutions are suitable for quality photographic prints, and the lower are suitable for e-mail inserts. For a digital portfolio, choose something in the middle (see the discussion of digital pictures below). Remember, the higher the resolution, the larger the size of the photo and the bigger the file size. Consider carefully before adding artifacts that are very large files because they may restrict the number of artifacts that can be added or they may take too long to open. In other words, save file space where possible.

You may want to (or need to, depending on the camera) process digital photos using a photo imaging program. Save photos as .jpg files; this format works best with Web pages and presentation software. Cameras vary in the options they provide for saving pictures. Some cameras allow saving in e-mail format, which provides smaller, lower-quality images that work well in a digital portfolio. Read the manual and take sample pictures in various resolutions.

Video Cameras

Video artifacts rivet the attention of portfolio reviewers, particularly if they cover critical events or illustrate a point well. If using a digital camcorder, download the video directly into the computer using a cable supplied with the camera. FireWire on the Mac or IEEE 1394 on a PC is a very fast external bus that is ideal for transferring video, and if both the camera and computer support it, the transfer is simple and relatively quick. If you do not use a digital video camera, you will need to convert the analog video to digital format using other hardware and software. Many still cameras are capable of making two- to three-minute videos. When using this option, check the manual to ensure that the camera's memory is sufficient for video.

CD Burner

To save work to a CD, you will need a CD recorder—sometimes called a CD burner because its laser beam selectively melts the recording layer of a CD. All recent computers have them. CD-R (compact disc-recordable) drives burn data to a CD until it is full, but it cannot be rewritten or reused. CD-RW (compact disc-rewriteable) drives rewrite data to a CD, like floppy disks did. Both CD formats hold 650–700 MB, but the physical structure of the discs is very different and not interchangeable. As you work, save to a CD-RW; however, if working on more than one computer, know that sometimes there are compatibility problems with CD-RW drives on different computers.

When the portfolio is complete and it is time to make copies for distribution, we recommend using a CD-R. This disc can be recorded on either a CD-R drive or a CD-R/RW drive. It also has a longer life than a CD-RW—thirty years as opposed to five years. But remember, as your experience grows, your portfolio will change.

Flash Drive

If using more than one computer to produce a portfolio—or if you desire a portable portfolio—purchase a flash drive. These thumb-sized, portable hard drives are recognized by any computer operating system that has the plug-and-play feature (Windows or Mac OS X). The drive plugs into a USB port, is recognized by the computer, and functions as a removable hard drive. Flash drives have capacities of 32 MB up to 64 GB, are readily available, and have become very reasonably priced. If the flash drive will be used to store video, we recommend a size of at least 2 GB.

Audio Recorder

Using audio files in the portfolio will necessitate either a digital audio recorder or an audio card and software that allow moving analog audio from tapes to digital files.

HOW DO I SAVE THE PORTFOLIO AS IT IS DEVELOPED?

While working on portfolios, links are created to connect elements in the portfolio. To ensure that the finished product works well, create a

DIGITAL FORMAT OPTIONS 45

filing system from the very beginning. A properly created filing system permits you to transfer the portfolio from one drive to another and from one computer to another and still know that the links all work. Creating links on a computer, involves setting the path to a file: drive:\folder\file (e.g., C:\portfoliodk\video1). If a file is later moved from one folder to another, all links to that file will need to be reset. To avoid this potentially arduous task, take time initially to plan the filing system. Whether using a computer hard drive, a flash drive, or a CD, the first task is to create a folder to hold everything:

1. If the folder is on a flash drive, double-click the My Computer icon on the desktop, then double-click the icon for the removable drive. If the folder will be on the desktop, simply leave the cursor on the desktop icon.
2. Right-click on the open space of either the flash drive list or the desktop.
3. Click File, scroll down to New and left-click.
4. From the options that appear, choose New Folder.
5. When the folder appears, the title New Folder will be highlighted. Type the new name and hit the Enter key.

Keep the folder name simple—your last name, "portfolio" plus your initials (no spaces), or something similarly distinctive. Every part of the portfolio should be in this folder. Create this folder once.

Next, create folders within this master folder. These secondary folders can be titled for standards (Standard1, Standard2, etc.) or for types of artifacts (e.g., Essays, Plans, Photos, Video). If the material is organized into standards folders, store video, pictures, or graphics in one central folder; this enables you to use a graphic in various parts of the portfolio while storing only one copy of it. Remember, only one copy of an artifact is necessary in the portfolio; you can link to that artifact from any place in the portfolio as long as you can locate it. Add folders as needed, and delete unused folders at any time.

Finally, fill the folders with artifacts and with elements for the portfolio. Keep file names simple and brief. When naming files, be sure that they are intuitively obvious; opening a document to determine what it contains breaks the creative flow of portfolio design. Because it is likely that school leaders may have more than one objective for each standard, code the objectives, activities, and artifacts by numbers and/or letters so that they associate with each other and are clearly identified. See Chapters 5, 6, and 7 for specific recommendations for labeling files.

HOW DO I USE PICTURES IN A DIGITAL PORTFOLIO?

First, when taking digital pictures, decide on the quality desired. Digital cameras allow a choice of resolution, and resolution determines quality. Resolution also affects the file size—the higher the resolution, the larger the file. Some cameras allow choosing the pixel size of an image (a megapixel equals more than a million pixels). For digital use, the smaller size, usually 640 by 480, is sufficient. If digital pictures are to be printed, it is best to use higher resolutions. Picture capture resolution of 1280 by 960 (1 megapixel), for example, will yield excellent quality 3-by-5 and 4-by-6 photographs. Picture capture resolutions of 1600 by 1200 (2 megapixels) or larger are required to yield photo quality 5-by-7 pictures.

If the camera offers resolution in terms of dots per inch (dpi), choose lower resolutions; computer screens usually display 72–100 dpi, whereas printers print 300 dpi or more. A lower resolution also produces an image that loads quickly and fits on the computer screen; pictures with higher resolutions often extend beyond the sides of the screen and cannot be viewed without scrolling. To include high-resolution pictures in the portfolio, bring the image into a photo-editing program and save it in a lower resolution.

Getting the images from a digital camera into a computer is easy. Although digital cameras store images on a variety of media (e.g., memory stick, Smart Media Card, MultiMedia Card), most digital cameras have USB or serial connections that allow direct transfer to the computer. Some computers have card readers that allow direct transfer; inserting the card is equivalent to inserting a flash drive. In some cases, the download can be initiated from the camera; in others, a photo editor is necessary to begin the download. Check the manual for the camera first.

Finally, remember that photo artifacts are more effective if they show action and if they show people doing something related to a standard; otherwise, the result is a scrapbook rather than a portfolio. Use a photo-editing program to crop the picture, adjust the brightness and contrast, and otherwise tinker with the image so that it effectively communicates what is desired.

HOW CAN I DIGITIZE AND USE 35 MILLIMETER PHOTOGRAPHS?

If there are only a few images, this is a job for a scanner. Check the scanner manual for operating instructions because scanners are either started by a button or launched from software. Some computers and scanners are configured to permit a choice of programs to scan a file; if the choice includes photo-editing software, use it and save a step. The software may ask what type of image is being scanned—color photo, grayscale, or line art. Black-and-white photos and newspaper photos are grayscale, and handwriting or black-and-white artwork are line art.

Launching the software that accompanies the scanner will often prescan the image. From the prescan, you select the area you want in a process similar to cropping a digital photo. Before clicking the Scan button, check the resolution setting (as with digital photos, the higher the resolution, the larger the photo and the larger the file) and the format. Formats for photos vary considerably. They include:

1. .jpeg—a compressed format with lots of color variation, which is particularly good for the Internet and for onscreen viewing;
2. .gif—good for onscreen viewing, best suited to line art and flat colors; much less color variation than .jpeg;
3. .tiff—a universal format that works on PCs and Macs; file sizes are usually quite large, and the format does not work on the Web;
4. .pict—a Mac-only uncompressed format dropped when Apple introduced OS X.

Once a photo is scanned into the computer, it can be manipulated just as if it were a photo taken with a digital camera. If planning to take more pictures with 35-mm film, there are a number of options for digitizing them. Most developers—from Kodak to the local drugstore—offer the option of obtaining photos on a picture CD in a number of different formats. Often, the CD also has software for editing the pictures. We recommend trying one of these CD services before committing to using it for portfolio photos.

HOW CAN I DIGITIZE AND USE VIDEOS ON A VHS TAPE?

Converting analog videos into digital videos requires a video digitizer (hardware) and a video-editing program (software). The digitizer can be built into the computer or it can be an external device. In either case, connect "video out" from the VCR or camcorder to the "video in" of the digitizer, using ordinary RCA cables. Adding a digitizer to a computer requires installing a video capture card into the CPU. A number of video cards are available for Windows systems, the most popular of which are made by Dazzle and Pinnacle Systems. Both of those cards come with video-editing software. Mac computers have digital video capability built into them, and both Mac and Windows include video-editing capabilities (*iMovie* on the Mac, *Movie Maker* on Windows XP, or downloaded *Windows Live Movie Maker* for Windows 7).

Editing involves bringing the video onto a storyboard, choosing the frames to be used, adding captions or voiceovers, and saving. One significant difference between professional videos and home videos is editing: professional videos are cut so that only the critical parts of the action are included, while home videos include everything. Emulate the pros by limiting video clips so they will load quickly and communicate effectively (so the viewer isn't tempted to end them prematurely). Clips should effectively address a standard in thirty to sixty seconds. Both Apple and Microsoft provide tutorials and helpful hints on their Web sites.

IS THE PROCESS OF USING A DIGITAL VIDEO CAMERA ANY DIFFERENT?

The process of downloading the video from the camera into the computer is different. Because the video is in digital format, it is ready to be moved to the computer, and most digital video recorders (including still cameras that take short videos) come with a FireWire or IEEE 1394 connection, which provides fast downloads. Check the connectors because FireWire connectors can have four or six pins. The correct cable makes it easy to connect the camera to the computer, run the software, and download the video. Be sure to edit the video for a more professional look and length.

WHICH SOFTWARE SHOULD I USE TO PRESENT THE PORTFOLIO?

If a school leader designs the portfolio, there are three main software choices: presentation software, Web editors, and online services. If the portfolio is being designed as part of a class or a program, the choice of software will often be determined by the class instructor or the college or university. Where there is a choice of software, that choice will be determined by the computer literacy of the portfolio designer. We address three software approaches to developing portfolios: presentation software, online services, and a Web page editor.

Presentation software is the most familiar, both for audiences and designers. Many computers come with PowerPoint (the most common presentation software program), and learning to use the program is fairly easy. Presentation software unifies the graphic theme for the portfolio and is designed to be viewed on a computer screen. A PowerPoint portfolio, in addition to including slides that highlight achievements or abilities, can perform other tasks, such as making links out of text or graphics on a slide; using links to launch other applications and display a document, picture, or video; linking slides with buttons (as Web sites link pages); and creating navigation buttons (e.g., Back, Next). Chapter 5 fully explores these various options.

When finished, the portfolio presentation can be saved with a viewer, and the audience does not need the program in order to view it. However, the audience will need the word processing program that produced the documents to view the presentation. It is possible to e-mail a portfolio created in presentation software; however, the portfolio folder must be compressed by the designer and then uncompressed by the recipient. Plan to save a portfolio done in presentation software in a medium (such as a CD) that can be handed to the recipient.

A second possible type of software to use is a Web editor. With a Web editor, you can create Web pages without knowledge of HTML (hypertext markup language), the computer language in which they are created. A Web page portfolio can be run on any computer that has a Web browser on it, which is virtually all computers. Web format is instantly recognizable to anyone who has used the Internet, and navigation of Web pages is second nature to most computer users. Most Web editors are "what you see is what you get (WYSIWYG)," and unless you are willing to learn the complexities of HTML, these are recommended. Simple Web editors are available for free download, and many computers have them as part of their software packages. Full-featured Web editors such as *Adobe Dreamweaver* and *Microsoft Expression Web* offer more capabilities, and more complexity; they can create Web pages with frames, they offer drag-and-drop functionality, and they include wizards that guide you through a good deal of the process. Linking documents, pictures, and video is relatively simple, and a Web page portfolio can also include links to the Internet. Documents in the portfolio can be run in their original programs (if the viewer's computer includes those programs) or they can easily be converted into HTML and displayed as Web pages.

A third software possibility is the online service. This book includes a subscription to two online services, TaskStream and LiveText. Instructions for accessing the TaskStream or LiveText account included with this text are provided in Chapters 6 and 7.

WHAT ARE THE ADVANTAGES AND DISADVANTAGES OF VARIOUS STORAGE MEDIA?

Many older computers have Zip drives or floppy disk drives. Both have virtually disappeared from current computers. While once the universal storage medium, the floppy disk has rapidly given way to CD, DVD, flash drive, and online storage, all of which hold much more than the 1.2 MB of a floppy.

A CD holds 650 MB of data. All current computers come with a CD/DVD drive, and a portfolio on CD would be accessible to anyone with a computer. In addition, it is possible to create a self-booting CD, so that it launches itself when placed in the drive. A CD can store Web pages or presentations, either of which can be run from the CD. This is an excellent medium for publishing and distributing the final portfolio, but it is not efficient for day-to-day storage and work.

Finally, if the portfolio is a Web page, it can be stored on an Internet server and accessed via the Internet. If the portfolio is created using an online service such as TaskStream or LiveText, it will be stored on the server of the online service. To post a Web page portfolio on the Internet, you will need a host (an Internet server that provides you space). Some schools and universities provide their employees and students with Web space to create Web pages.

Free Web space is also available from a number of Internet hosts. To get the space, you have to agree that your page will include the host's advertisements (the host controls ad content). If you use a site with free hosting, first access a page hosted at the site to see that it loads quickly and that it includes appropriate ads. A final option is to pay a host for your Web page portfolio. A quick search of the Internet will provide you with thousands of possibilities.

ACTIVITY

Preparing a digital portfolio requires various technology skills. In the development of a digital portfolio, it is essential that you assess your technology skill level. The technology self-assessment is designed to provide insight into those skills. You may access the technology self-assessment at http://tiny.cc/Digital_Portfolio for those using PowerPoint (Supplemental Resources) and through either TaskStream (Supplemental Resources) or LiveText (Supplemental Resources).

Following each skill is a rating scale ranging from beginning (1–3), competent (4–6), to expert (7–10). You may total the responses by hand or download the digital version of the self-assessment to your computer. Once you have downloaded the self-assessment, you can complete and save the self-assessment to your computer. The downloaded version of the document will tabulate the total score for you.

Item Interpretation

A rating below four on any item indicates a need for additional instruction in that area. While that learning may extend the time required for producing a digital portfolio, the resultant portfolio will be stronger, thanks to a more diverse set of artifacts, clearer organization, and smoother functionality. A rating between four and six indicates competence in a given area but also room for further learning and growth. A rating between seven and ten indicates expert skill in that given technology area and no need for additional learning or growth.

For the overall rating, a total score between 28 and 84 indicates "beginning" technology skill development. Readers with a "beginning" score need to consider the standards-based digital portfolio project as an opportunity to achieve significant learning and growth along the five technology skill dimensions. It is important to identify which items and dimensions warrant special attention and to seek out assistance either through various online tutorials, software classes or seminars, or assistance from colleagues and critical friends.

A total score between 85 and 168 indicates overall "competence" among the five technology skill dimensions. In this instance, it is important to identify the very specific dimensions or items that warrant additional learning and to seek out assistance through the various sources as previously indicated. A total score between 169 and 280 indicates that the respondent is an "expert" and may identify those dimensions or items that might warrant additional growth.

Readers whose overall total is "competent" or "expert" should strongly consider the TaskStream or LiveText version of the digital portfolio. Since TaskStream and LiveText provide more technology options, they are more suitable for technologically skilled readers. A total score of "beginning" suggests that the reader may be more comfortable using the PowerPoint version. Readers selecting the PowerPoint version are familiar with the Microsoft Office suite of software, but are not skilled in using the Internet or other software programs.

DIGITAL FORMAT OPTIONS   53

SUMMARY

Choosing which software to use is a very important decision. Review the following requirements for PowerPoint, TaskStream, and LiveText based on your needs, abilities, and willingness to try new approaches.

PowerPoint requires:

1. familiarity with word processing and graphics,
2. distribution of a CD by mail or other physical means,
3. more storage space for the final product,
4. preparing a list of standards for hyperlinks,
5. learning and using built-in hypermedia features, and
6. a viewer's computer having programs in which to view artifacts.

TaskStream and LiveText require:

1. familiarity with using the Internet,
2. distribution via the World Wide Web,
3. no local storage space for the final product,
4. linking to standards lists provided by TaskStream or LiveText,
5. hypermedia linking provided by TaskStream or LiveText, and
6. programs for viewing artifacts are generally compatible with Web pages.

5

THE POWERPOINT OPTION

Chapter 4 culminated in an activity in which you selected one of three preferred digital format options: PowerPoint, TaskStream, or LiveText. Chapter 5 is written specifically for those who select PowerPoint as the preferred standards-based digital portfolio tool. This chapter also reviews basic Microsoft Office PowerPoint 2007 functions and steps to begin assembling your standards-based digital portfolio.

REVIEW OF BASIC POWERPOINT FUNCTIONS

We do not provide basic technology training, but we suggest how technology can be used when developing a standards-based digital portfolio. Therefore, this chapter does not provide PowerPoint training. If you have questions about using and modifying the outline template, refer to the PowerPoint Help files or Microsoft's online PowerPoint training at http://office.microsoft.com/en-us/powerpoint/default.aspx. In addition, Montgomery and Wiley (2004, 2008) provide a thorough exploration of PowerPoint functions. PowerPoint is a graphics presentation program included in the Microsoft Office suite of programs.

Review the software and hardware configurations on your computer because variations can affect functionality. In particular, earlier versions of PowerPoint might not run files produced on later versions, but later versions will typically run files produced on earlier versions. To open PowerPoint, turn the computer on, left-click on the Start button at the bottom left corner of the screen, place the cursor over the text, All Programs, scroll to PowerPoint 2007, and left-click.

You can also open PowerPoint by creating a shortcut on the screen desktop. To create a shortcut to PowerPoint, click on the Start button at the bottom left of the screen, left-click on All Programs, left-click on Microsoft Office, right-click on Microsoft Office PowerPoint 2007, and left-click on Create Shortcut.

ACCESSING THE STANDARDS-BASED SCHOOL LEADER DIGITAL PORTFOLIO TEMPLATE

First, create a folder for the digital portfolio project files, including the School Leader Portfolio Template and all digital artifacts. This folder is particularly important for making copies of the portfolio for review. Unless the artifacts and the PowerPoint presentation are in the same folder, reviewers can access the PowerPoint presentation but not the artifacts. To create a folder, right-click in an open area of the desktop. Scroll down to New, and left-click on Folder. A New Folder icon will appear. Place the cursor in the text field under the icon and backspace to erase the text and rename the file.

A template for the School Leader Portfolio can be found at http://tiny.cc/Digital_Portfolio. Type the URL into your browser's URL window and click the Enter key. At the site, click on Digital Portfolio Resources, then on OPEN HERE to access PowerPoint, then on the folder titled OPENSchool Leader Portfolio TEMPLATE in PowerPoint. Once the PowerPoint file is open, save a copy of the file for your own use as follows: select File in the menu bar, scroll down and left-click on Save As, select the folder in which the file is to be saved in the Save In field, rename in the File name field, and left-click once on the Save icon.

ADDING OBJECTIVES, ACTIVITIES, AND ARTIFACTS TO THE DIGITAL PORTFOLIO

The central components of the portfolio are the objectives, activities, and artifacts documented for each standard. One way to construct the portfolio is provided below. Prior to adding objectives, activities, and artifacts to the digital portfolio, complete the worksheets available at http://tiny.cc/Digital_Portfolio. The ISLLC 2008 Examples-Worksheets file and the NETS-A 2009 Examples-Worksheets file are located through the Supplemental Resources link. Each file contains a worksheet for each standard and a completed sample of that worksheet. Open and save each of these files under a new file name, either on a flash drive or on your computer hard drive.

For the following illustration, we assume the ISLLC 2008 Examples-Worksheets are saved on the hard drive as My ISLLC 2008 Worksheets, and the NETS-A 2009 Examples-Worksheets are saved on the hard drive as My NETS-A 2009 Worksheets. To add the text for objectives and activities, copy and paste to the School Leader Digital Portfolio as follows:

1. Complete and save My ISLLC 2008 and My NETS-A 2009 Worksheets.
2. Open the file and select the completed worksheet. Place the cursor in the desired column at the beginning of text that is to be added. Holding down the left mouse button, scroll and highlight the text.
3. Left-click the Edit menu and left-click on Copy.
4. Open your School Leader Digital Portfolio. Left-click once on the View menu to make sure the file is in Normal View.
5. In the Outline or Slide Screen in the left inset box, select the slide for the desired standard.
6. Place the cursor immediately after the word Objectives or Activities where the text is to be added. Left-click once and a gray highlighted box will appear indicating that the selected area of the slide can be edited.
7. Click on the Edit menu, scroll down, and click on Paste. If the pasted typeface appears much larger, highlight the selected text

and select 16-point or other desired font size in the formatting tool bar above the slide.

More than likely, you will have more than one objective for the standards and should code the objectives, activities, and artifacts by numbers and letters so that they are clearly identified. For example, the first objective under any given standard can be labeled "1," the second objective "2," and so on. If there are two activities associated with objective 1, they can be labeled "1.A" and "1.B." If there are two artifacts associated with activity 1.A, they can be labeled "1.A.1" and "1.A.2." If there are three artifacts for activity 1.B, they can be labeled "1.B.1," "1.B.2," and "1.B.3."

Most objectives and activities are text, but artifacts could be text or image files. Remember to add artifacts to the digital portfolio so that viewers will clearly understand what they are viewing and how it relates to the selected standard, objective, and activity. Because of the need to orient the viewer, the Artifacts section of each standard requires more careful planning and assembly.

The process for adding various types of artifacts to the digital portfolio is as follows:

1. Open the file and select the completed worksheet. Place the cursor in the artifact column at the beginning of the designated text. Holding down the left mouse button, scroll and highlight the text to be copied.
2. Left-click on Edit and left-click on Copy.
3. Open the School Leader digital Portfolio. Left-click once on the View icon to make sure the file is in Normal View.
4. In the Outline or Slide Screen in the left inset box, select the slide and the chosen standard.
5. Place the cursor immediately after the word Artifacts for the text to be added. Left-click once and a gray highlighted box will appear indicating that the selected area of the slide can be edited. Left-click the Edit menu and left-click on Paste. If the pasted typeface appears much larger, highlight the text and select 16-point or other desired font size in the formatting tool bar above the slide.

Linking the artifact text label to a text or image file or Web site is accomplished as follows. Left-click and highlight the artifact text label that is to be hyperlinked. Right-click and select the Hyperlink icon in the scroll bar. In the inset box that appears, select the location of the file in the Look In field. Select the main portfolio project folder. Left-click on the selected file (the name of the file will appear in the Address field). Left-click OK.

Develop a system of labeling and filing artifacts so they can be easily accessed and added to the digital portfolio. Notice that under the icon Introductory Text, text from the ISLLC 2008 Worksheet was pasted in the Header Text field, like the process for Objectives and Activities. As a reminder, the artifact is "1.A.1" so it is clear to which objective and activity the artifact is related.

PUBLISHING AND SHARING YOUR PORTFOLIO

There are many ways to publish and share a digital portfolio created in PowerPoint. We recommend three options. Each option has advantages and disadvantages. First, the digital portfolio can be shared by saving the PowerPoint presentation and artifacts to a CD. There are two types of CDs: CD-RW and CD-R (see Chapter 4 for an explanation of the differences in these two). Assemble the digital portfolio and artifacts by burning files to the CD-RW, which can then be altered. However, the CD-RW is severely limited due to computer software and hardware compatibility issues. Therefore, the CD-RW can be used to assemble but not share the digital portfolio. Once the portfolio is assembled on the hard drive or CD-RW, it can be burned on to a CD-R. The CD-R has fewer hardware and software compatibility issues. However, it also cannot be altered or changed once burned; therefore, it is essential that the digital portfolio be complete, including all artifacts, prior to burning on to a CD-R.

A second option is using a USB flash drive. These data-storage devices, plugged into a USB port, are well suited for sharing digital portfolios and have few hardware or software compatibility issues.

A third option is publishing or sharing the digital portfolio to the Internet by uploading the PowerPoint and digital artifacts to a Web page.

This is most easily accomplished through the use of Web-page authoring software. TaskStream and LiveText, described in the following chapters, are examples of this technique. There are many issues with publishing and sharing a digital portfolio to the Web, including confidentiality of material and fair use.

ACTIVITY

Complete the formative evaluation rubric (available on the CD) at several stages while developing the digital portfolio. Each time you complete the rubric, have a critical friend complete it as well. Compare and contrast these responses. Identify strengths and opportunities for improvement. Develop strategies to address improvement needs. Identify issues and concerns and explore these with a critical friend.

SUMMARY

In this chapter, PowerPoint was presented as an option to create the standards-based school leader digital portfolio. You received instructions for accessing and using the PowerPoint template and sample completed portfolio (on the enclosed CD). Within PowerPoint, you can access the standards-based school leader digital portfolio template; modify the portfolio outline; add objectives, activities, and artifacts; and share the portfolio. You are now prepared to assemble the standards-based digital portfolio in PowerPoint.

THE TASKSTREAM OPTION

Chapter 4 culminated in an activity in which you selected one of three preferred digital format options: PowerPoint, TaskStream, or LiveText. This chapter is written specifically for those who select TaskStream as the preferred standards-based digital portfolio tool.

USING TASKSTREAM

In this chapter, we suggest how TaskStream, an online service, can be used to develop a standards-based digital portfolio. We do not provide training for using TaskStream. You may request a demonstration of the software prior to making a decision to subscribe to TaskStream. To request a free demonstration of the software, log on to TaskStream at https://www.taskstream.com/pub/ and click the Request Demo link on the homepage under Learning Achievement Tools. Follow the directions and complete the required steps on the subsequent pages to receive the demonstration account (see Figure 6.1).

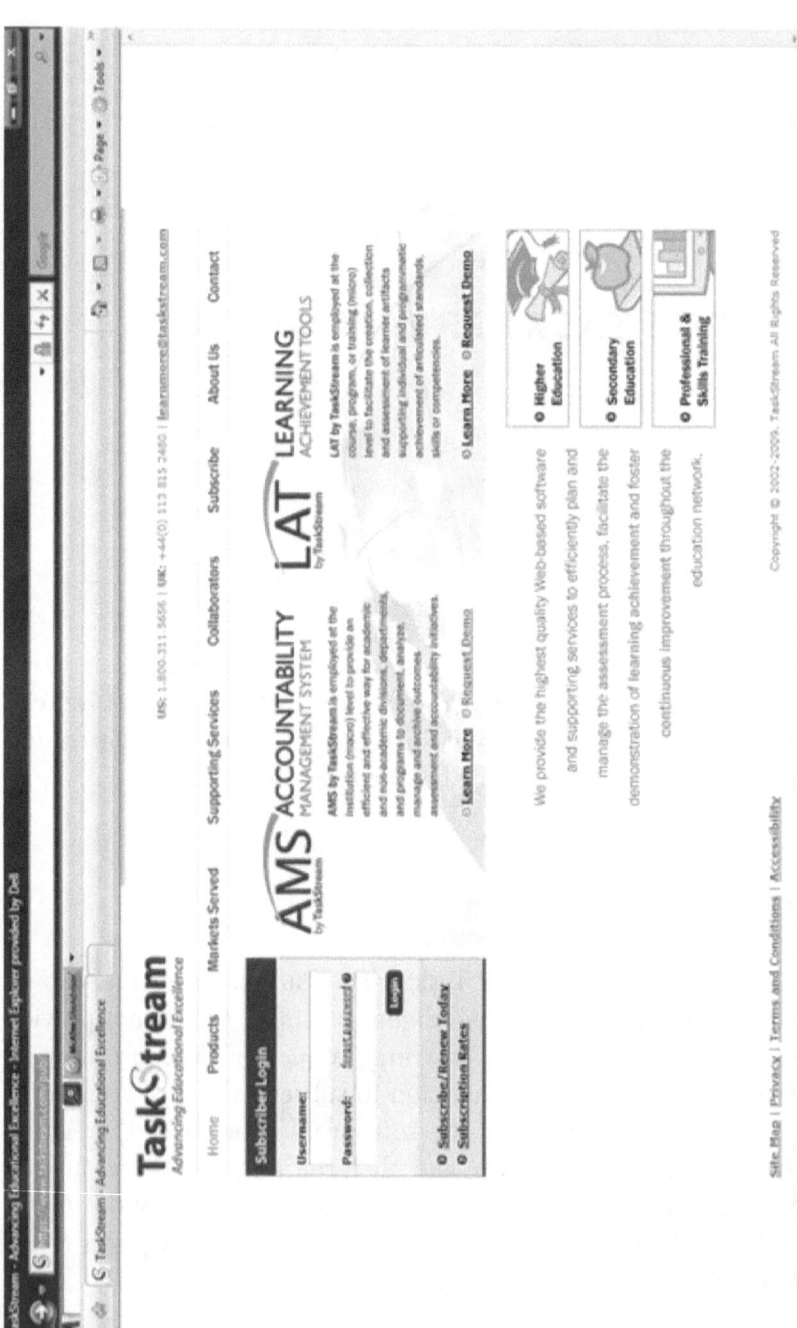

Figure 6.1. TaskStream Homepage Screen

A SUBSCRIPTION TO TASKSTREAM AND THIS TEXT

To access the TaskStream subscription included with this text, go to http://tiny.cc.Digital_Portfolio, click on Digital Portfolio Resources, then click on "OPEN HERE for instructions to access TaskStream," then click on TaskStream Key Code. Using this code to open a subscription to TaskStream will give you access to the school leader standards-based digital portfolio template, the school leader standards-based sample portfolio, and other tools. Complete the following steps to subscribe and set up your account. Please note that because the Web site is frequently revised, the following screens might look somewhat different.

1. Go to the TaskStream homepage at https://www.taskstream.com/pub/ and click the Subscribe/Renew Today link on the left center of the screen. See Figure 6.1.
2. Under Step 1, Activate Subscription, you are given a choice to Create, Renew, or Convert My Guest Account. See Figure 6.2. Select Create a new TaskStream subscription. Under option 2 enter the key code. The key code may be obtained by logging on to http://tiny.cc/Digital_Portfolio, clicking on Digital Portfolio Resources, clicking on OPEN HERE for instructions to access TaskStream, and clicking on TaskStream Key Code.doc. Click the Continue button. Complete the following steps to access the sample template.
3. Complete steps 2–4 to finish the registration process. Do not hesitate to contact TaskStream's Mentoring Services if you encounter any difficulties subscribing.

After creating your TaskStream account, if you have questions about how to use the outline template, refer to the TaskStream Help Index on the Web site; it includes a vast collection of online and downloadable support materials. To access the Help Index, click the Help link located at the top right-hand corner of the screen. See Figure 6.3. From this page, click the Downloadable Guides link on the right, then the Folios & Web Pages link under the topic Instructional Design to obtain a guide to assist you with the creation of a digital portfolio. Note that Adobe Acrobat Reader is required to access this and other guides

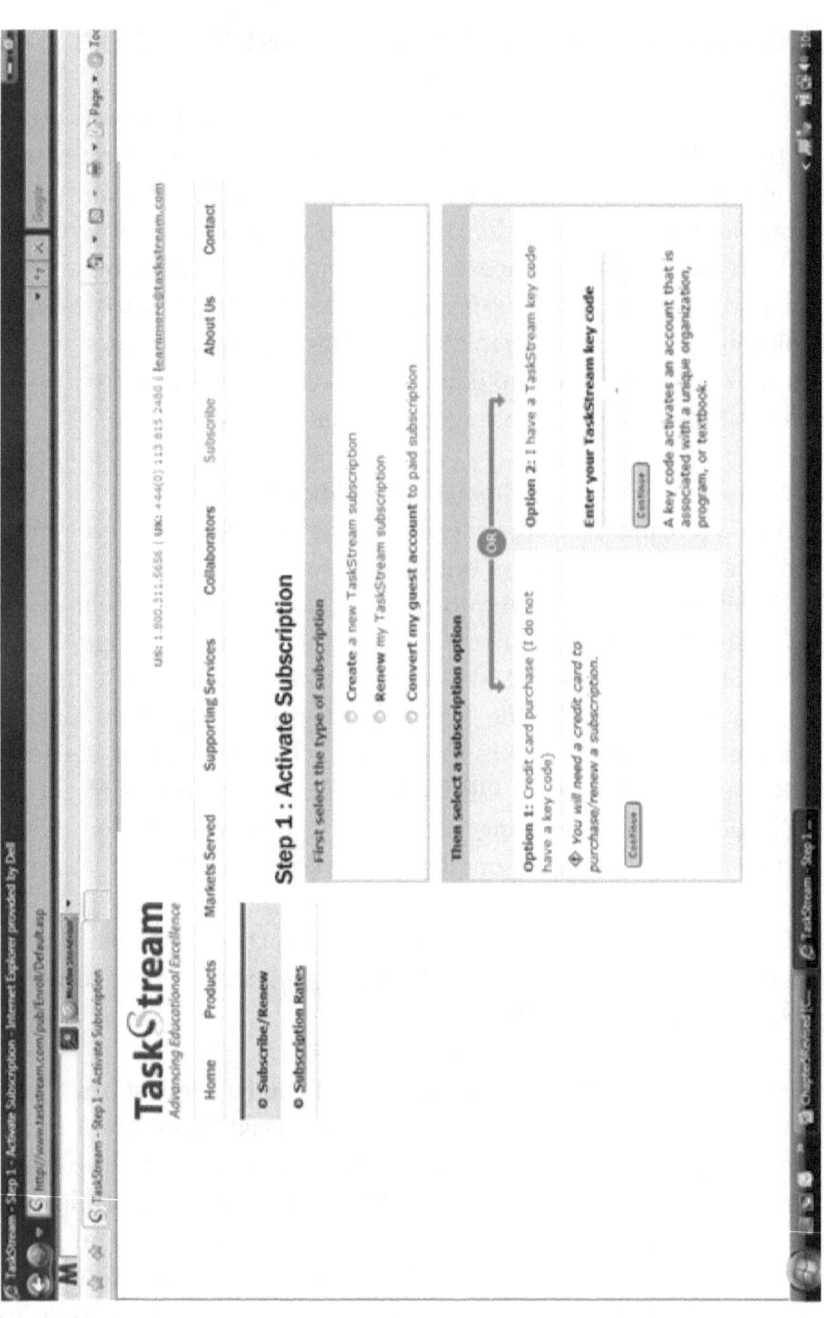

Figure 6.2. TaskStream Activate Subscription Screen

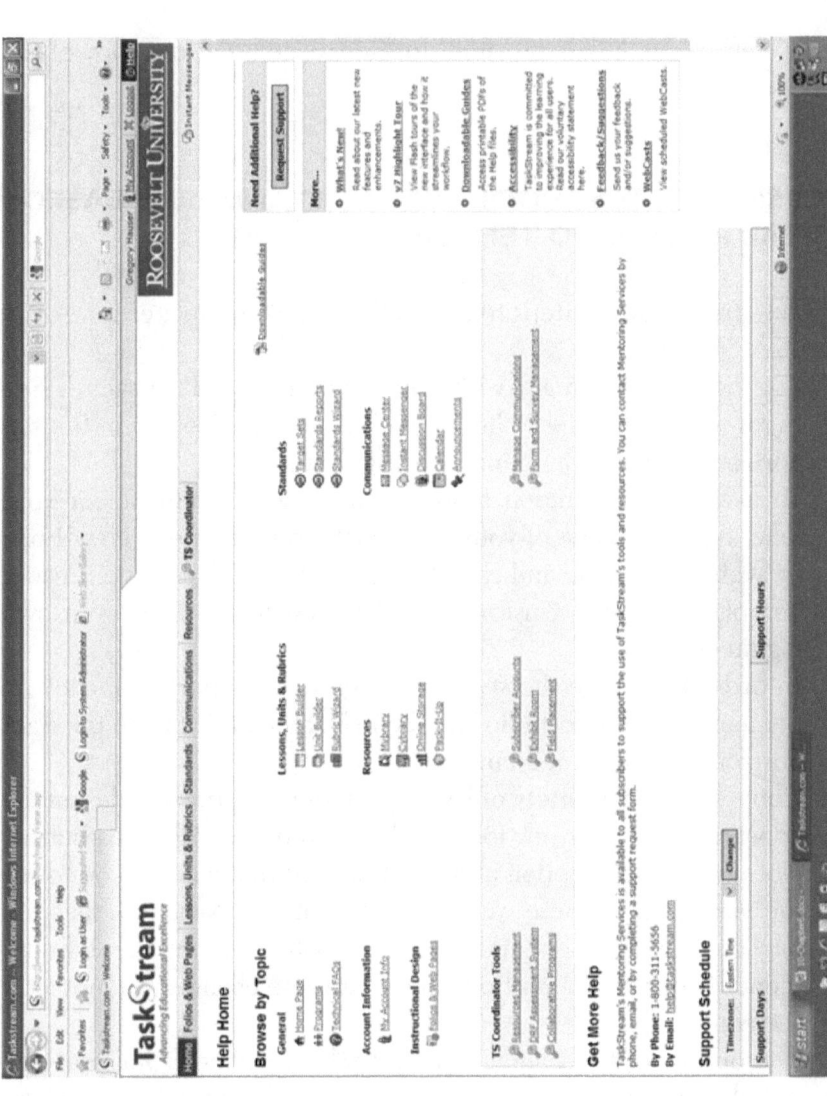

Figure 6.3. TaskStream Help Index

on the Web site. A link is provided for downloading a free copy of the Adobe software.

ACCESSING THE SCHOOL LEADER STANDARDS-BASED DIGITAL PORTFOLIO TEMPLATE

Complete the following steps to access the sample template:

1. Log on to TaskStream with your username and password. See Figure 6.1. Click the Folios & Web Pages link located in the top horizontal navigation menu. See Figure 6.4.
2. To use the presentation folio School Leader Template for your folio, type the name of your new portfolio in the field, New Folio or Web Page Name and click Continue. Select the School Leader Template from the Custom Templates list to construct your own digital portfolio.
3. In order to change the style or design of your portfolio, click on the name of your portfolio and then click the Style tab on the right horizontal navigation menu.
4. Choose among a variety of layout and theme options to design the appearance of your portfolio, and click the Save Changes button. Note the preview option at the bottom left that enables you to see the Web-view of these various configurations. Note too, that you may change the layout and theme at any time during the development of your digital portfolio and that these changes will not alter the content.
5. The outline of the standards-based school leader digital portfolio template is visible in the vertical column on the left side of the screen. You can edit the structure of the outline by adding, deleting, moving, or copying a page. See Figure 6.5.

ADD, DELETE, MOVE, AND COPY PAGES AND SECTIONS

Log on and click on the Folios and Web Pages icon on the horizontal navigation menu, then select the portfolio you have created using the

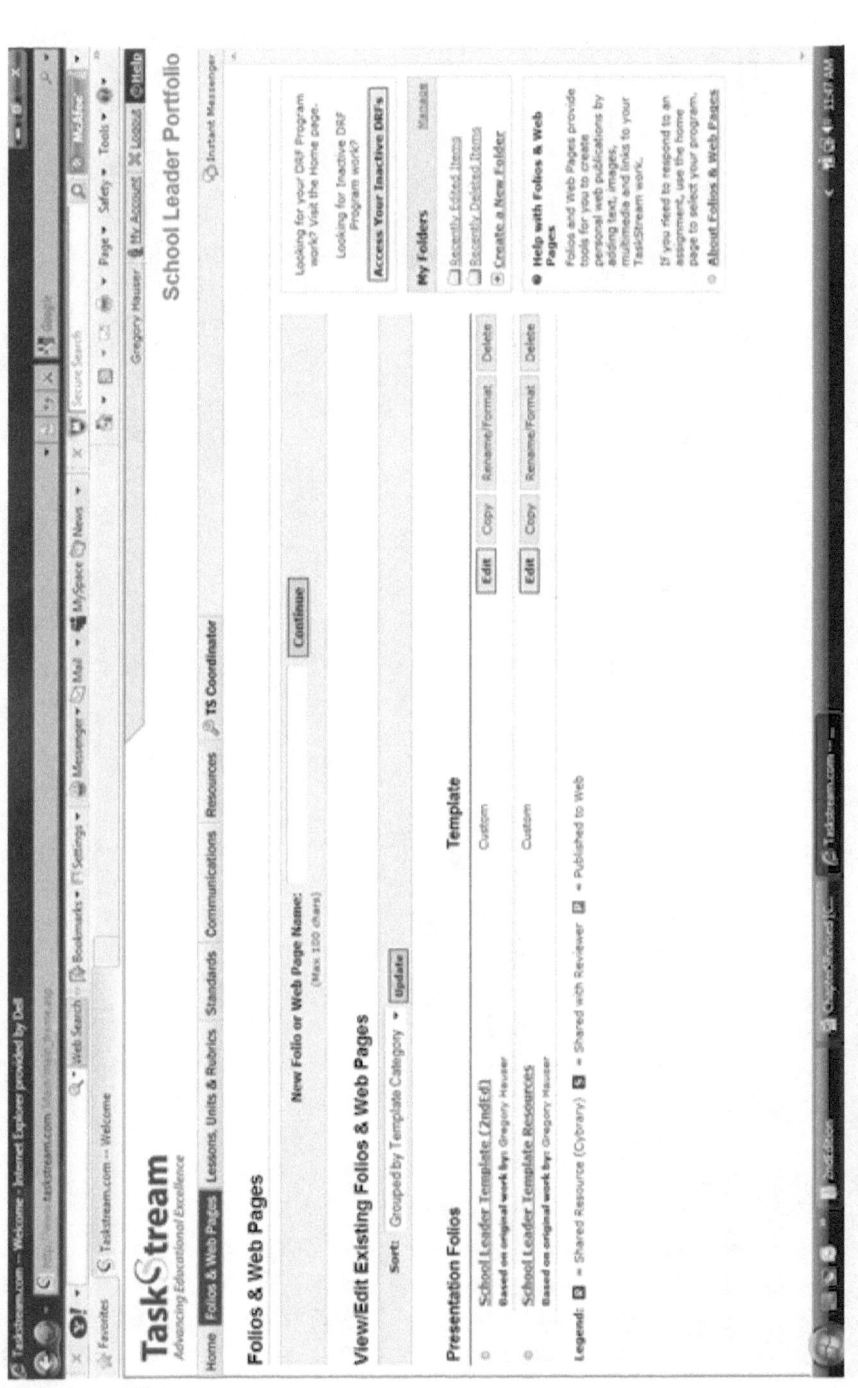

Figure 6.4. School Leader Template

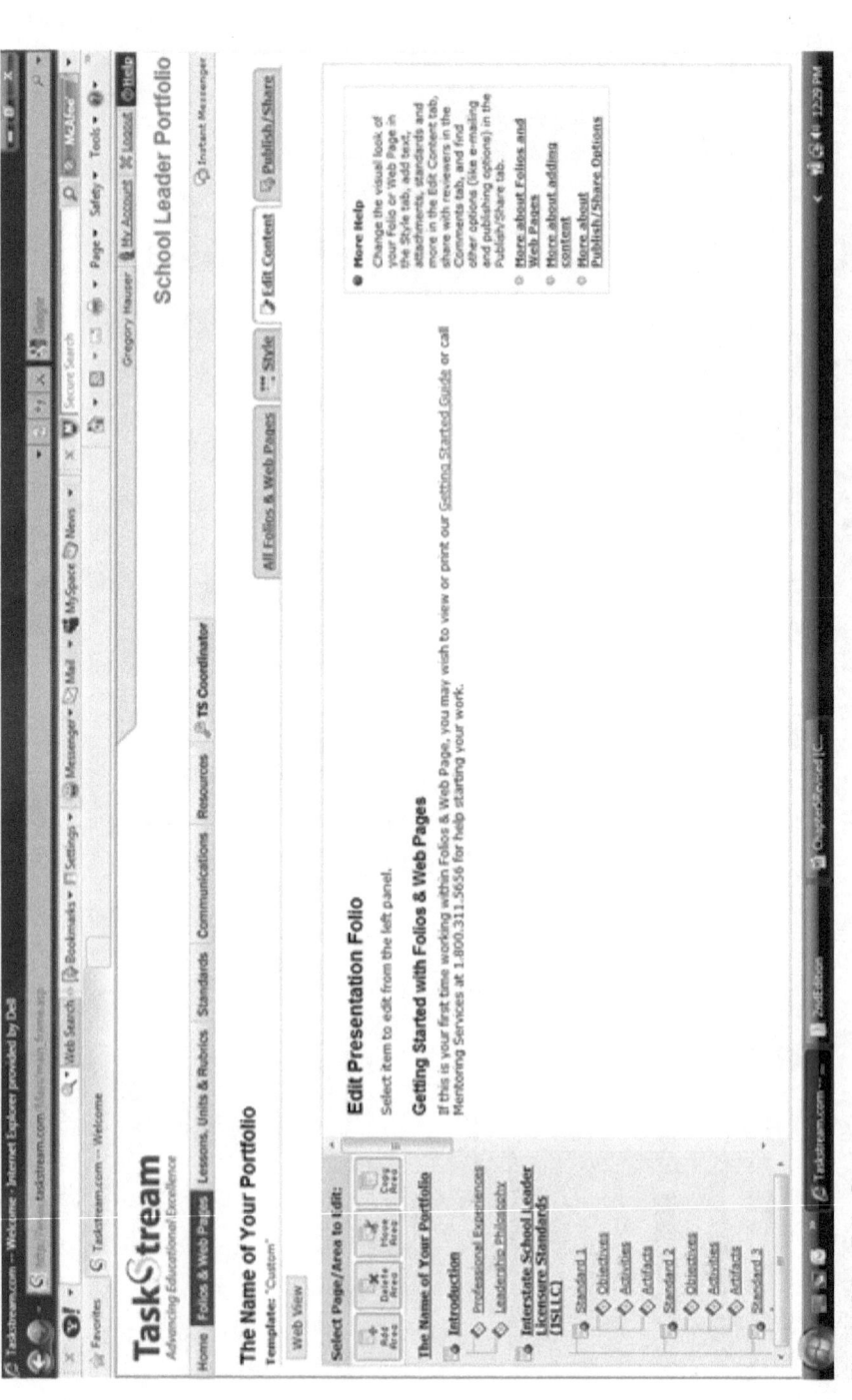

Figure 6.5. Edit Content

School Leader Template. You can add, delete, move, and copy pages and sections of the portfolio outline using the edit features in the left frame of the screen below. Note that a page icon is identified as a page with a small globe on the bottom right-hand side, and a section icon is identified as a small diamond. Scroll down the taskbar to the right of the Edit Structure frame and select an area of the portfolio to modify. When selected, the page/section icon will be highlighted.

1. To add a page, click on the page or section of the outline to be modified. Then click the Add Page button from the top of the Edit Structure frame. In the example below, the page could be added to follow the Introduction or as a page linked to the Introduction page. Complete the title, descriptor, and placement fields as desired and then click Create. See Figure 6.6.
2. To add a new content section to a page, click on the selected page in the outline. The steps are similar to adding a new page. Note the horizontal Add menu at the lower middle of the screen. Click the Section icon on the far lower right hand portion of the screen. Complete the title and descriptor fields and click Create.
3. You can also edit the content of sections by clicking on the Text and Image button on the bottom of the page. The horizontal menu at the bottom of the page also provides the option to add additional content, including text and images, slideshows, standards, main text, attachments, video, links, and reports. See the horizontal menu at the bottom of the page.

ADD OBJECTIVES, ACTIVITIES, AND ARTIFACTS TO THE DIGITAL PORTFOLIO

The central components of portfolios are the documented objectives, activities, and artifacts for each standard. One suggested strategy for constructing the portfolio is provided below. Note that the example objectives, activities, and artifacts for the ISLLC 2008 and NETS-A 2009 Standards are included in the School Leader Sample Portfolio. Prior to adding objectives, activities, and artifacts to the digital portfolio, complete the standards worksheets. The ISLLC 2008 Examples Worksheets

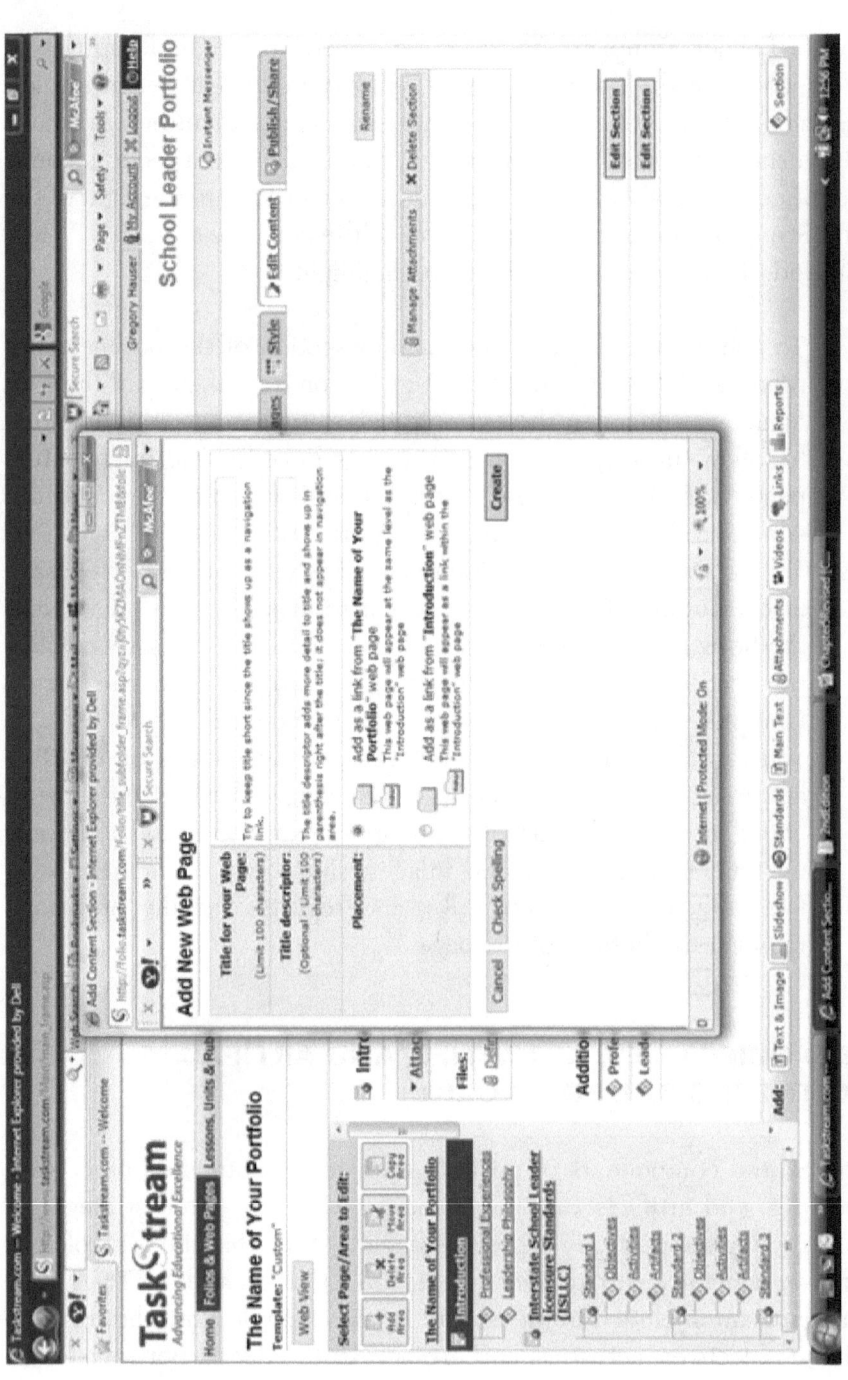

Figure 6.6. Add a Page

file and the NETS-A 2009 Examples and Worksheets file are located in the Supplemental Resources section of the Outline of the School Leader Template. Open and save each of these files under a new file name, either on a flash drive or computer hard drive.

For the following illustration, we assume that the ISLLC 2008 Examples and Worksheets are saved on the hard drive as My ISLLC 2008 Worksheets and the NETS-A 2009 Examples and Worksheets are saved on the hard drive as My NETS-A 2009 Worksheets. Once the worksheets are completed, add the text for the objectives and activities to the School Leader Digital Portfolio. The following three sections describe how to add materials to the Sample Portfolio.

Adding Objectives to the Digital Portfolio

For this task, two programs run simultaneously and you toggle from one to the other using the buttons on the Task Bar at the bottom of the computer screen. Log on to TaskStream and open your School Leader Digital Portfolio. Then open the completed My ISLLC 2008 Worksheets file in your word processor; select the desired text from the Objectives column, and under the Edit menu, select Copy. Switch to TaskStream and click on the Objectives section of the selected standard in the outline field. See Figure 6.7.

Note the horizontal navigation menu at the bottom of the page. For the purpose of adding objectives to your portfolio, we recommend using the Main text option as the preferred method of adding text. Click on the Main text icon. Place the cursor in the blank field, right-click, and select Paste. The text will appear in the box. Again, if you have more than one objective for the standards, code by numbers and letters for clear identification (see the completed sample digital portfolio for examples). Add the designated label in front of the text in the Add/Edit Main Text for Objectives field, and click the Save and Return button at the bottom right of the window.

You may also add content to your objectives through the following functions: text and image, slideshow, standards, main text, attachments, videos, links, and reports. Each of these tabs provides a variety of options for adding content to the portfolio. The other functions may be more usefully applied when adding activities and artifacts. See Figure 6.8.

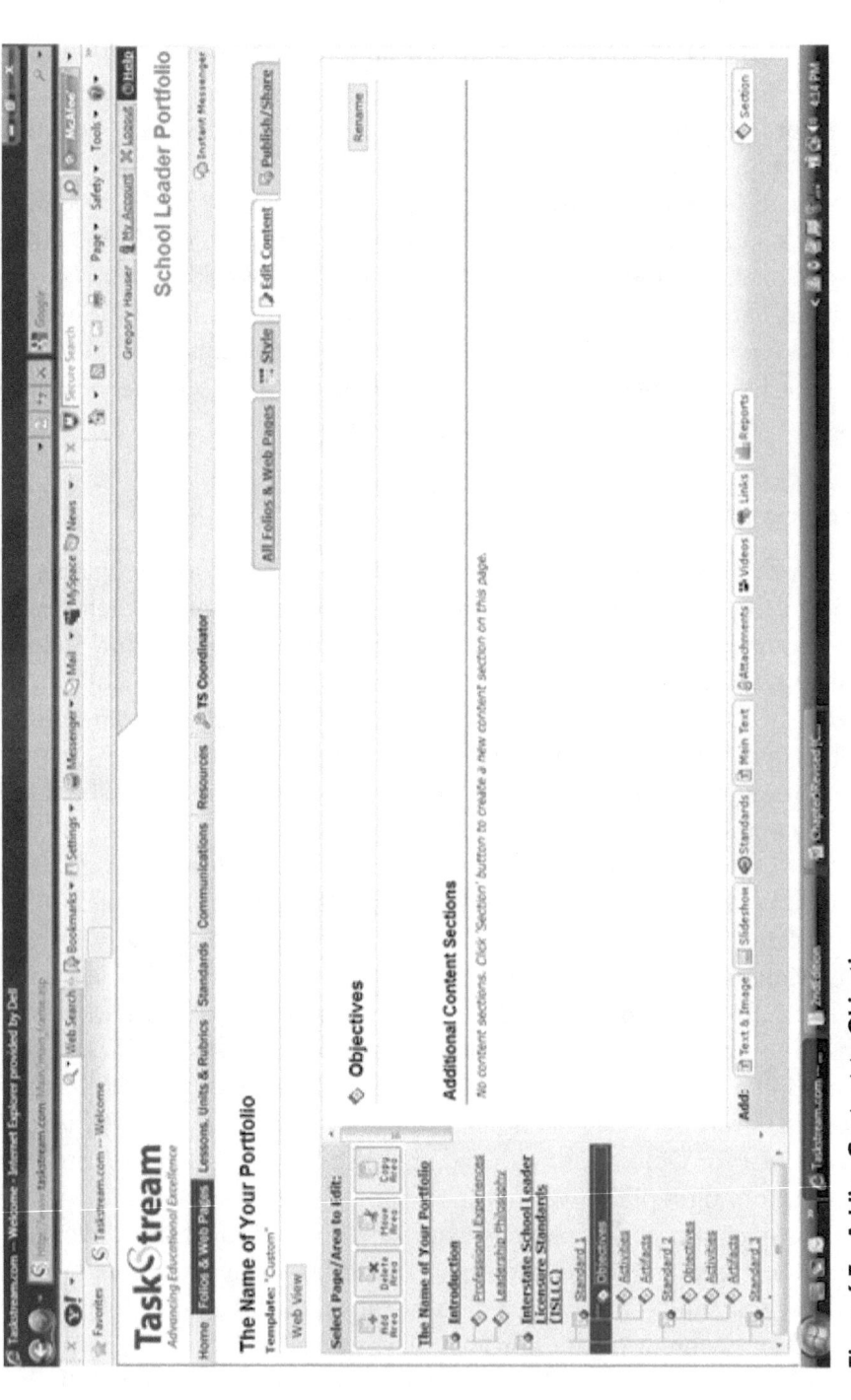

Figure 6.7. Adding Content to Objectives

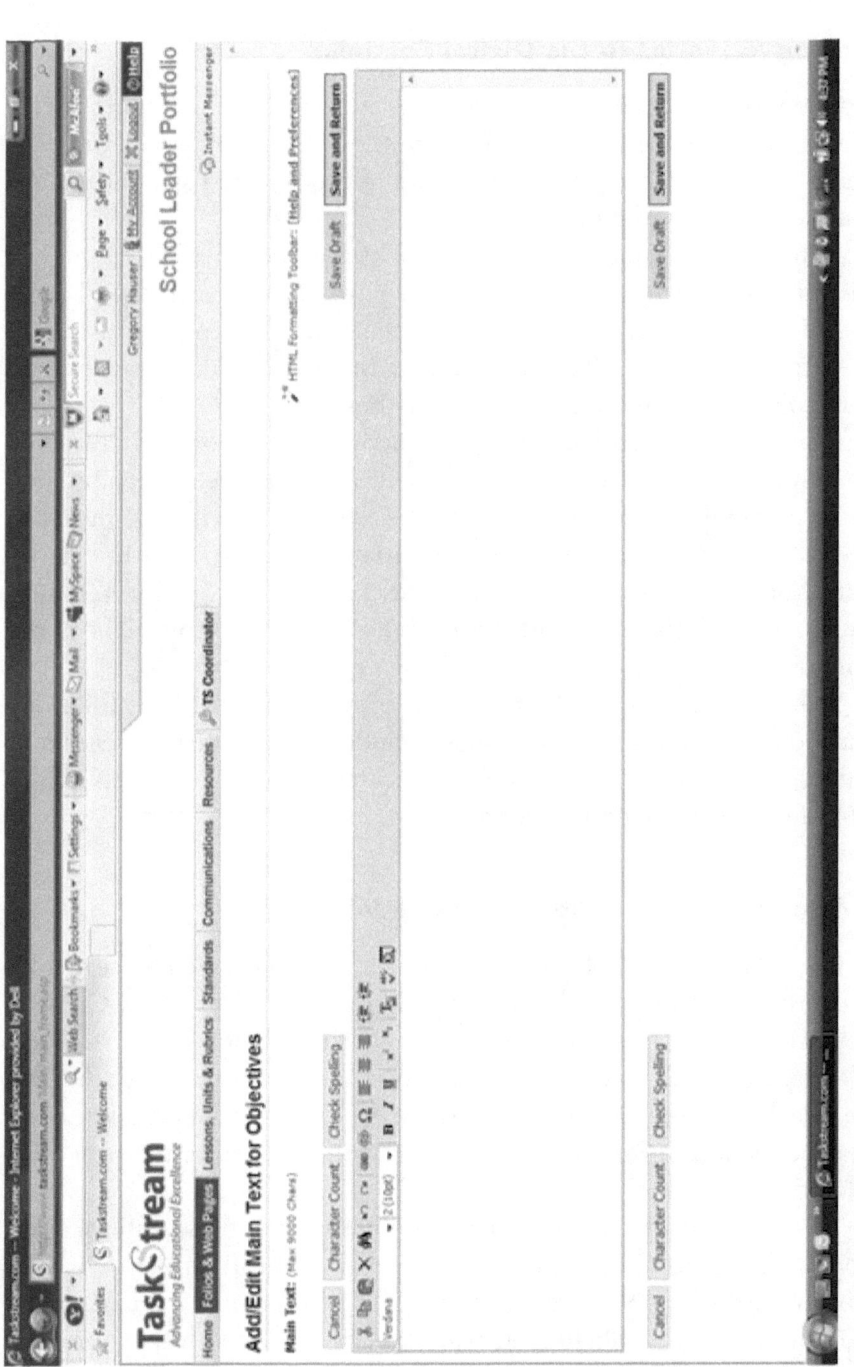

Figure 6.8. Add/Edit Objectives

Adding Activities to the Digital Portfolio

Open My ISLLC 2008 Worksheets file. Select the required text under the Activities column, and from the Edit menu, select Copy. In TaskStream, click the Activities section of the selected standard in the outline field. See Figure 6.9.

Note the horizontal navigation menu at the bottom of the page. For the purpose of adding activities to your portfolio, we recommend using the Main text option as the preferred method of adding text. Click on the Main text button. Place the cursor in the blank field, right-click, and select Paste. The text will appear in the box.

Again, if you have more than one activity for each standard, code by numbers and letters for clear identification (see the completed sample digital portfolio for examples). Label the activities so that they are clearly identified with the appropriate objective. Add the designated label in front of the text in the Add/Edit Main Text for Activities field, and click the Save and Return button at the bottom right of the window.

You may also add content to your activities through the following functions: text and image, slideshow, standards, main text, attachments, videos, links, and reports. Each of these tabs provides a variety of options for adding content to the portfolio.

Adding Artifacts to the Digital Portfolio

Open My ISLLC 2008 Worksheets file. Select the chosen text from the Artifacts column, and under the Edit menu, select Copy. Click on the Artifacts section of the selected standard in the outline field. Most often artifacts will consist of documents of one kind or another that can be attached to the portfolio. For these types of artifacts, click the Attachments button from the row of tabs at the bottom of the page. See Figure 6.10.

To add a new attachment, select the file from the three options available, namely, from a file saved on your computer, flash drive, or CD; from a previously uploaded file; or from artifacts created in TaskStream. For the most part, attachments will likely be uploaded from your computer. Name your file in the field provided. You may also provide a

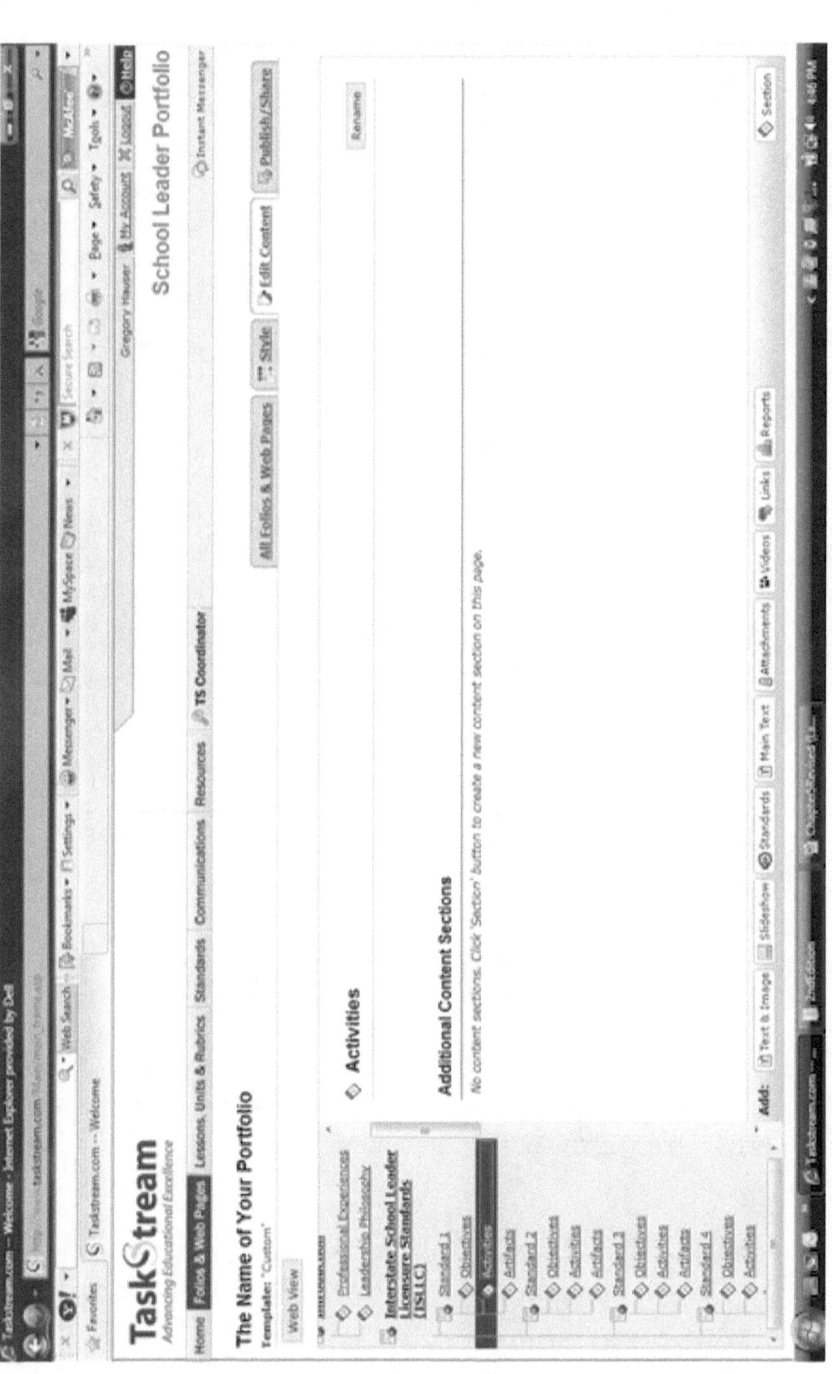

Figure 6.9. Adding Activities

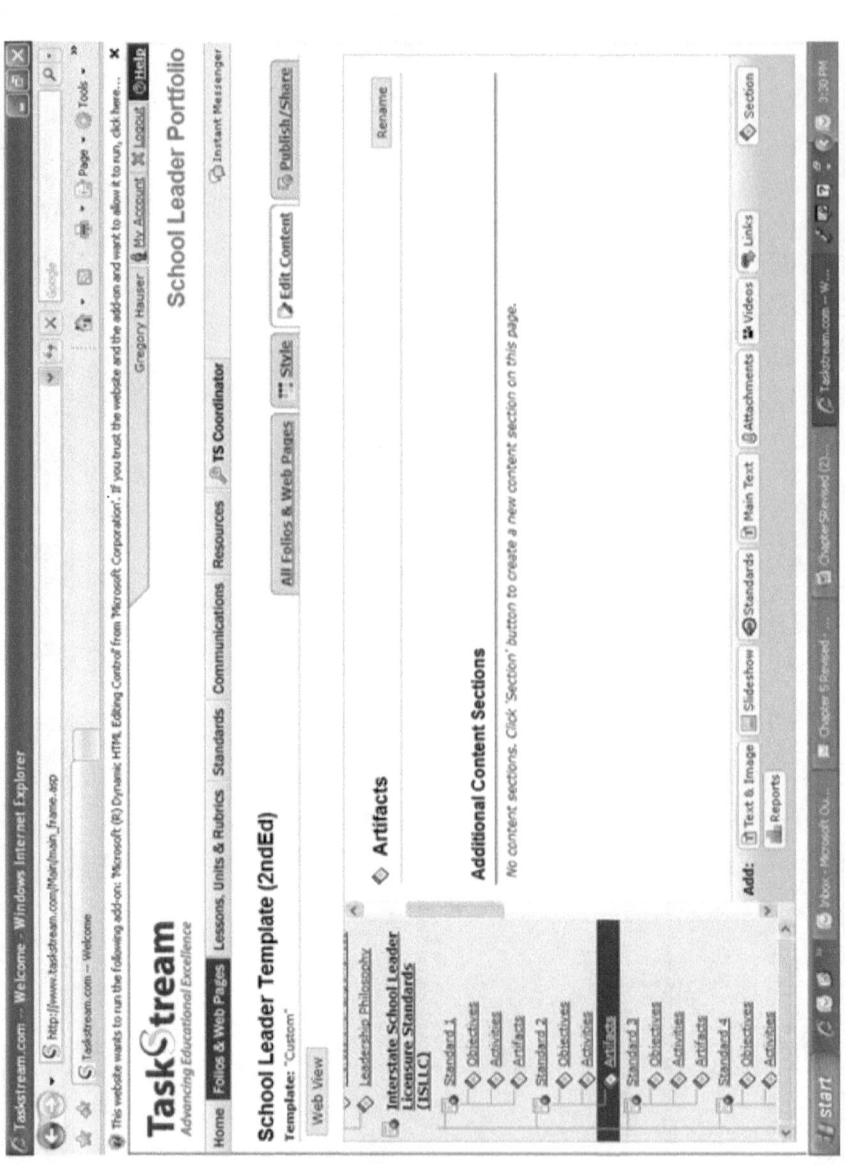

Figure 6.10. Adding Artifacts

THE TASKSTREAM OPTION

description of your attachment; however, if the file is carefully labeled, this will likely not be necessary. The option, Attach Standards, is not necessary as the outline of the portfolio is already included with the ISLLC 2008 Standards.

In addition to adding various documents as attachments, you can also add images and text, slideshows, videos, Internet links, as well as reports. See Figure 6.10 and the row of icons on the bottom of the page. You can add images by clicking on the text and images icon. Select images from the stock images provided in TaskStream or from another source (a hard drive, flash drive, or CD). Please note that there is a 512 K or .5 MB size limit for each image that you upload. Each image may be formatted for both placement and size. The image may be placed either at the right, left, or center of the page, and the image may also be sized as either large, medium, or small. Click the Save and Return button after you have selected and formatted an image.

Slideshows and images may be added as artifacts by clicking on the Slideshow icon from the row of tabs at the bottom of the page. On the left side of the screen you may add a slideshow single image; however, the image must be either a GIF or JPG file (ending with the .gif or .jpg extension). To add a slideshow, enter the title of the slideshow in the field provided in the center of the page and select the slideshow from your computer, flash drive, or CD by using the browse option. Click Save and Return when finished.

Video may be added to the portfolio by selecting the Video icon from the row of buttons at the bottom of the page. Select a video from your computer and name the file. You may limit the play length of the video and provide a brief description.

Links may be added as artifacts by clicking on the Links icon from the row of buttons at the bottom of the page. Name the link in the field provided and enter the URL in the select link field below. You may also create a link from an existing page in the portfolio to another through a drop down menu.

The reports option from the row of buttons at the bottom of the page does not function without special permission from the TaskStream coordinator at your institution (school, district, college, or university).

You should consider using a wide range of artifacts. Please note, however, that artifacts need supplemental information to provide context for viewers to understand what they are viewing and how it relates to the selected standard, objective, and activity. Therefore, the Artifacts section of each standard requires thorough planning and assembly. Refer to the ISLLC Standard 4, Artifact 1.A.1 example in the School Leader Sample Portfolio. Notice that under the Introductory Text tab, the text from the ISLLC Worksheet was pasted in the Introductory Text field by the same process for objectives and activities. Examine the School Leader Sample Portfolio for other examples of how you can add artifacts to a portfolio.

ACCESS AND REVIEW OF THE SAMPLE DIGITAL PORTFOLIO

To access and review your portfolio:

1. Log on to TaskStream with your username and password. Click the Resources button in the top navigation menu. Select the Go to Cybrary link in the Cybrary area. Search for the School Leader Sample Portfolio by clicking the Advanced Search button, then searching for School Leader Sample Portfolio by keyword. See Figure 6.11.
2. Click on the name of the School Leader Sample Portfolio from the resulting list. The sample portfolio includes example objectives, activities, and artifacts for ISLLC 2008 and NETS-A 2009 Standards from the planning worksheets. See Figure 6.12.

ACTIVITY

Complete the formative evaluation rubric (see Supplemental Resources on TaskStream) at various times during the development process. Each time, have a critical friend complete the rubric as well. Compare and contrast these responses. Identify strengths and opportunities for improvement. Develop strategies for improvement. Identify issues and concerns and explore these with a critical friend.

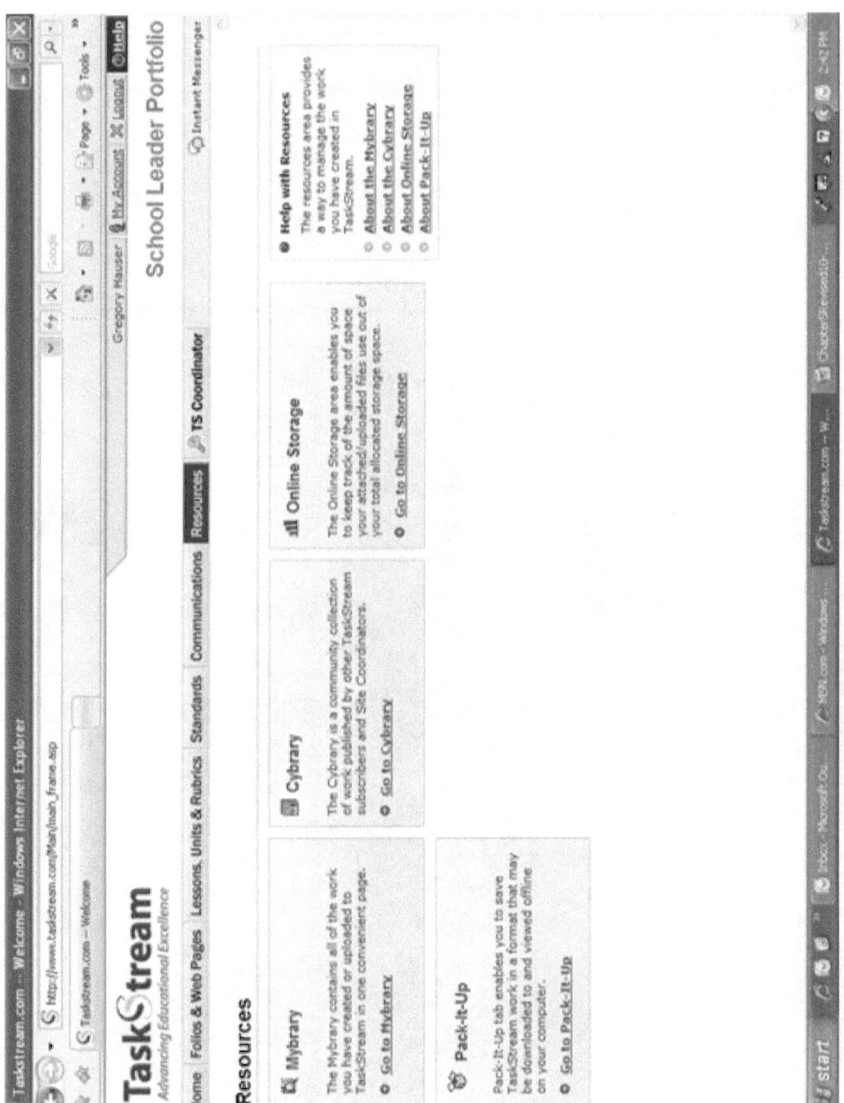

Figure 6.11. Cybrary

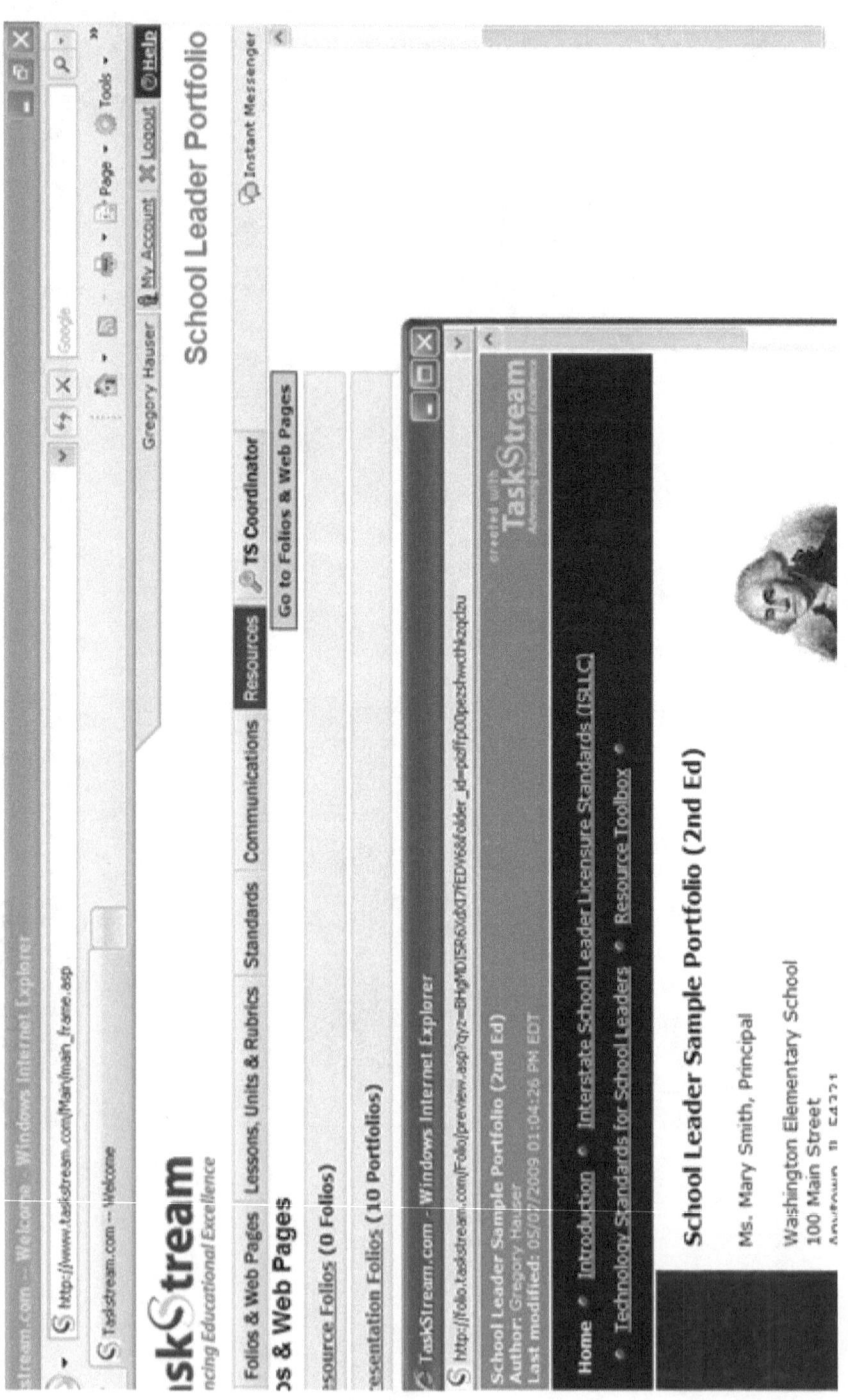

Figure 6.12. School Leader Sample Portfolio

SUMMARY

In this chapter, the TaskStream online portfolio option was presented. The process of logging on, registering, and subscribing to TaskStream is a matter of following the screen prompts. Within TaskStream, you can access the standards-based school leader digital portfolio template; modify the portfolio outline; and add objectives, activities, and artifacts. You are now prepared to assemble the standards-based digital portfolio in TaskStream.

7

THE LIVETEXT OPTION

Chapter 4 culminated in an activity in which you selected one of three preferred digital format options: PowerPoint, TaskStream, or LiveText. This chapter is written specifically for those who select LiveText as the preferred standards-based digital portfolio tool.

USING LIVETEXT

In this chapter, we suggest how LiveText, an online service, can be used to develop a standards-based digital portfolio. Just as we do not provide training for TaskStream, we do not provide training for LiveText. You may request a demonstration of the software prior to making a decision to subscribe to LiveText. To request a free demonstration of the software log on to LiveText at https://www.livetext.com/ and click the green-colored Request a Demo button in the center of the homepage, or e-mail support@livetext.com. Follow the directions and complete the required steps on the subsequent pages to receive the demonstration account. See Figure 7.1.

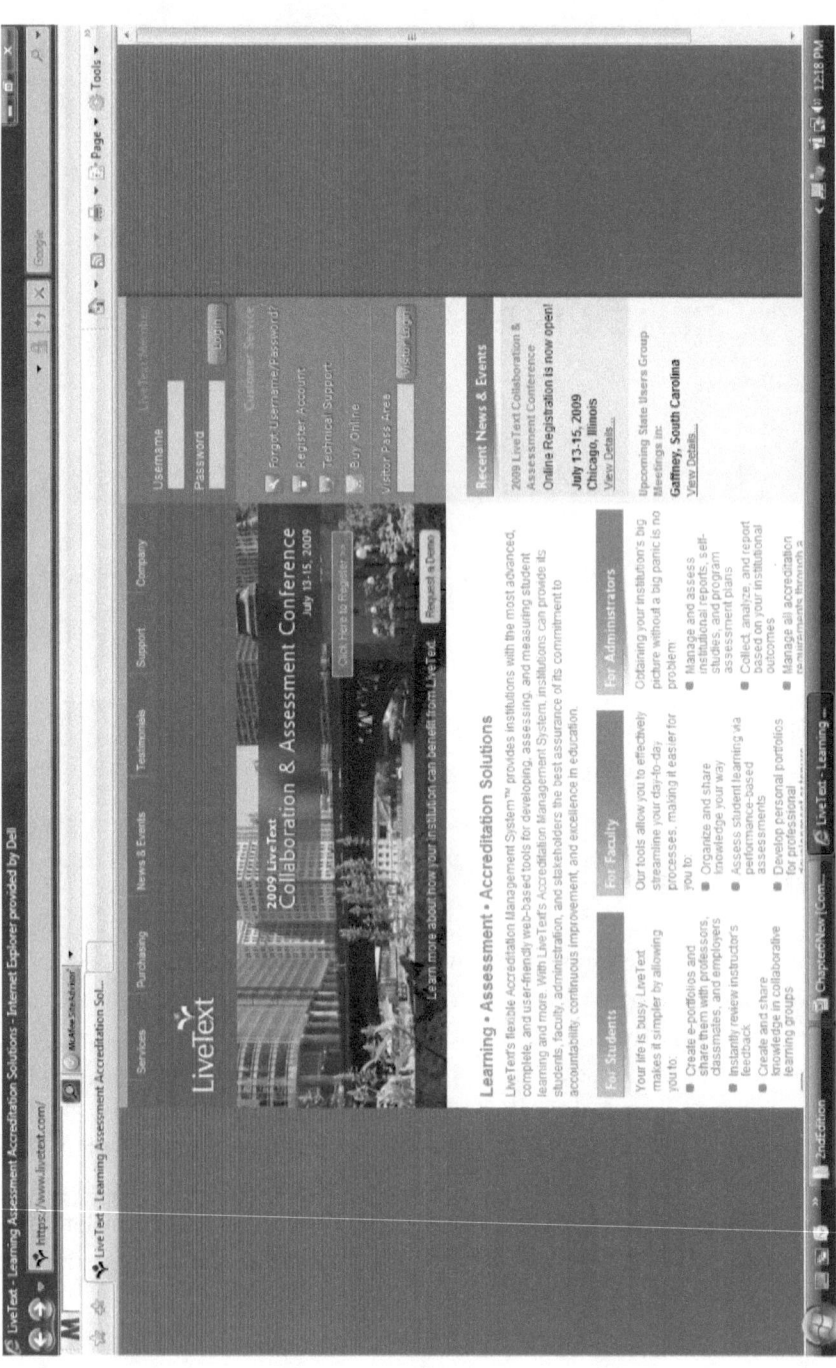

Figure 7.1. LiveText Homepage Screen

ACCESSING THE LIVETEXT SUBSCRIPTION

The purchase of this text and a subscription to LiveText includes access to the school leader standards-based digital portfolio template, the school leader standards-based sample portfolio, and other tools. Contact LiveText via e-mail at accounting@livetext.com, or by telephone at (866) 548-3839 for distribution of a key code associated with this textbook. The key code will grant the user access to templates and tools created in LiveText for use in conjunction with this textbook.

Complete the following steps to subscribe and set up your account. Please note that because the Web site is frequently revised, the following screens might change.

1. Go to the LiveText homepage at https://www.livetext.com/ and click the Purchasing button on the left center of the screen. See Figure 7.1.
2. Under the heading, How Do I Get Started?, you are provided with four membership options, namely, student membership, faculty membership, professional membership, and institution purchase. Please carefully review this section if you are unclear regarding which membership option is appropriate. See Figure 7.2. Choose the student, faculty, or professional option and enter the key code supplied by LiveText to activate your account. Only one subscriber can use the code. Please note that it is essential that readers enter the appropriate key code accompanying the text in order to access the portfolio template and other tools described in this handbook.
3. Click the Register Account link in the customer service area on the right side of the LiveText homepage.
4. Enter the key code provided by LiveText.
5. Click the Next button to go to the next step.
6. Enter all required information on the Personal Information page.
7. Click the Next button to go to the next step.
8. You will be prompted to create your username and password. When creating a username, the name will be compared to all LiveText users. If you get a message stating "Username is already taken," you will have to modify your username for it to be accepted.

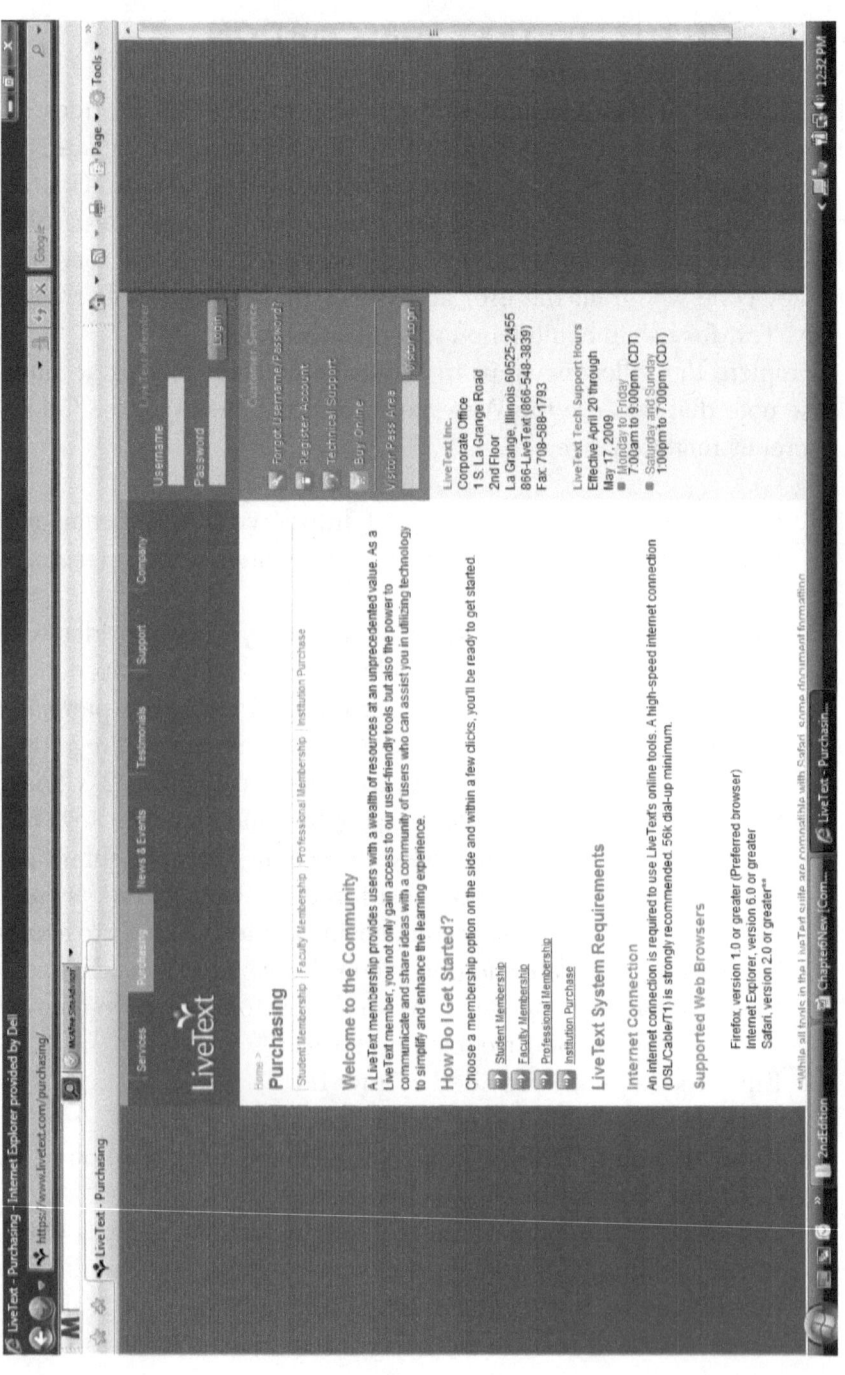

Figure 7.2. Choose a Membership

9. Click the Next button to go to the next step.
10. On the Confirmation page, you can edit your information by clicking on the Edit buttons in each section.
11. Select the Terms of Service check box.
12. Click the Confirm button to complete the registration process.
13. After you successfully complete the registration process, LiveText will display the Account Activation Confirmation page. This page will display your newly created username and password. Your login information will also be sent to the e-mail address provided during account registration.

Do not hesitate to contact LiveText's Technical Support services if you encounter any difficulties with the subscription process. After creating your LiveText account, if you have questions about how to use the outline template, contact LiveText in one of three ways: (1) enter your query at the LiveText homepage under Technical Support; (2) access the Quick Guide Help link at https://www.livetext.com/c1_help/quickguides/; (3) either e-mail or telephone for assistance through the Support icon at the top of the homepage.

ACCESSING THE SCHOOL LEADER STANDARDS-BASED DIGITAL PORTFOLIO TEMPLATE

Complete the following steps to access the sample template:

1. Log on to LiveText with your username and password. See Figure 7.1.
2. From the Dashboard page click on the Documents icon in the toolbar at the top of the page. See Figure 7.3.
3. Click on the New button on the left-hand side of the lower toolbar.
4. In the Folder field, choose the Template option. In the Template field, select Standards-Based Digital Portfolio. See Figure 7.4.
5. Enter a Title for your standards-based digital portfolio.
6. Enter a Description at your discretion.
7. Click the Save a New Document button located on the lower right side below the Template Outline. See Figure 7.4.

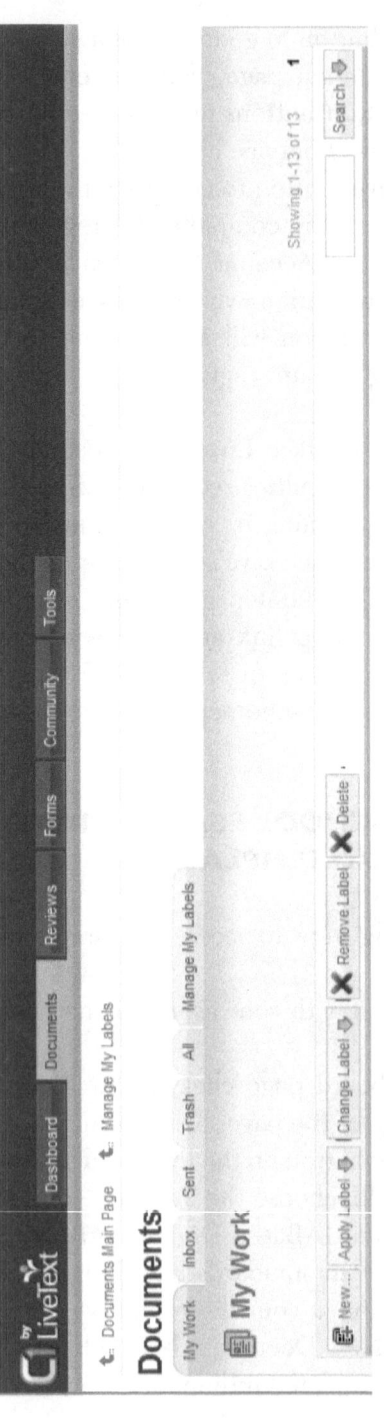

Figure 7.3. Dashboard

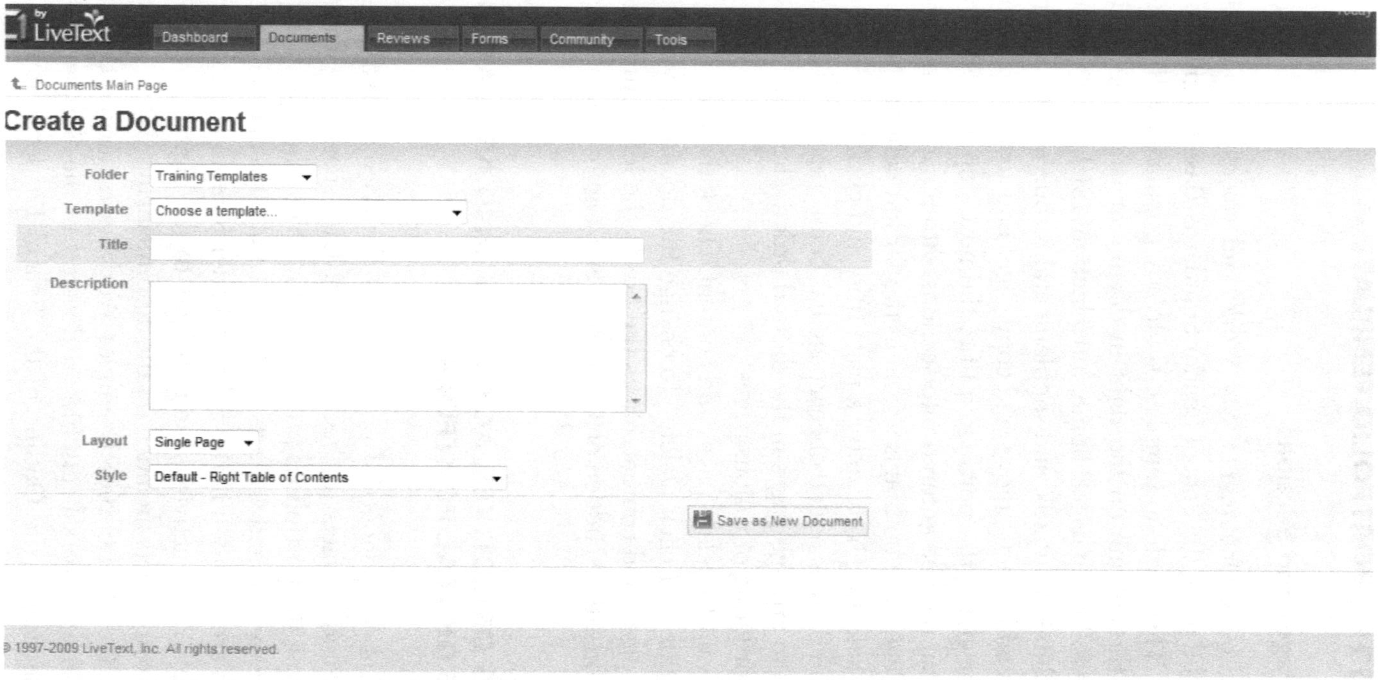

Figure 7.4. Standards-Based Digital Portfolio Template

EDITING THE PORTFOLIO TEMPLATE

Adding Pages and Sections

Log on, click Documents, My Work, and select the portfolio you have created using the School Leader Standards-Based Digital Portfolio Template. The portfolio template is already populated with an outline visible in the column on the right in document view. The outline includes the following pages: home, introduction, ISLLC 2008 Standards, NETS-A 2009 Standards, and supplemental resources. See Figure 7.5.

You can add, delete, move, and copy pages and sections to your portfolio. After giving the portfolio a title, the next step is to add content. Content can only be entered into sections within pages. Under the tab Manage Pages, the outline is visible in the far left column. You can add a page by selecting New, enter a page title, and click OK. Sections and content can then be added once a page has been created. Click the Page Order tab to arrange pages in the desired order. The arrow icons allow for the reordering of various pages.

If you want to delete pages and content, check the box to the left of the page title and click Delete. To change the document view but not eliminate pages and content, check the box to the left of the page title, and click on either Hidden or Unhidden. See Figure 7.6.

ADDING OBJECTIVES, ACTIVITIES, AND ARTIFACTS TO THE DIGITAL PORTFOLIO

The central components of portfolios are the documented objectives, activities, and artifacts for each standard. One suggested strategy for constructing the portfolio is provided below. Note that the example objectives, activities, and artifacts for the ISLLC 2008 and NETS-A 2009 Standards are included in the School Leader Sample Portfolio. Prior to adding objectives, activities, and artifacts to the digital portfolio, complete the worksheets included on the accompanying CD or available on LiveText. The ISLLC 2008 Examples-Worksheets file and the NETS-A 2009 Examples-Worksheets file are located in the Supplemental Resources section of the Outline of the School Leader Template. Open

Figure 7.5. Standards-Based Digital Portfolio Document View

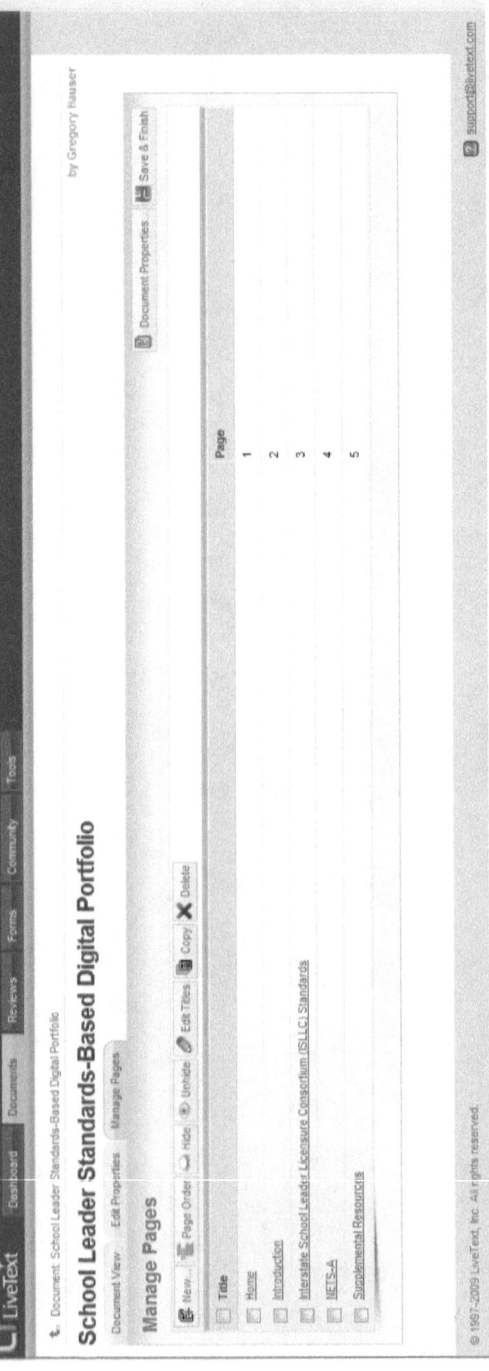

Figure 7.6. School Leader Standards-Based Digital Portfolio Template

and save each of these files under a new file name, either on a flash drive, CD, or computer hard drive.

For the following illustration, we assume that the ISLLC 2008 Examples-Worksheets are saved on the hard drive as My ISLLC 2008 Worksheets and the NETS-A 2009 Examples-Worksheets are saved on the hard drive as My NETS-A 2009 Worksheets. Once the worksheets are completed, add the text for the objectives and activities to the School Leader Digital Portfolio. The following three sections describe how to add materials to the Sample Portfolio.

Adding Objectives to the Digital Portfolio

For this task, two programs run simultaneously and you toggle from one to the other using the buttons on the Task Bar at the bottom of the computer screen. Log on to LiveText and open your School Leader Digital Portfolio. Then open the completed My ISLLC 2008 Worksheets file in your word processor; select the desired text from the Objectives column, and under the Edit menu, select Copy. Switch to LiveText, select the portfolio document, and under the Table of Contents column on the far right, select the ISLLC 2008 Standards. Click on the desired standard. There is a page associated with each standard. You may add content to the page associated with each standard. See Figure 7.7.

Content may be added to the Objectives section of a standard as follows. Click the Edit button to the right of the section. See Figure 7.8.

Add the desired text related to the objective by copying and pasting from the worksheets or word processing the text directly into the Section Editor field. Note that you can modify the text through various word processing features built into the software. If you have more than one objective for any given standard, code by numbers and letters for clear identification (see the completed sample digital portfolio for examples). The objectives should all be included in the Section Editor field. Click the Save and Finish icon when you have finished adding the objective. You can save changes as you proceed by clicking the Save Changes icon. See Figure 7.9.

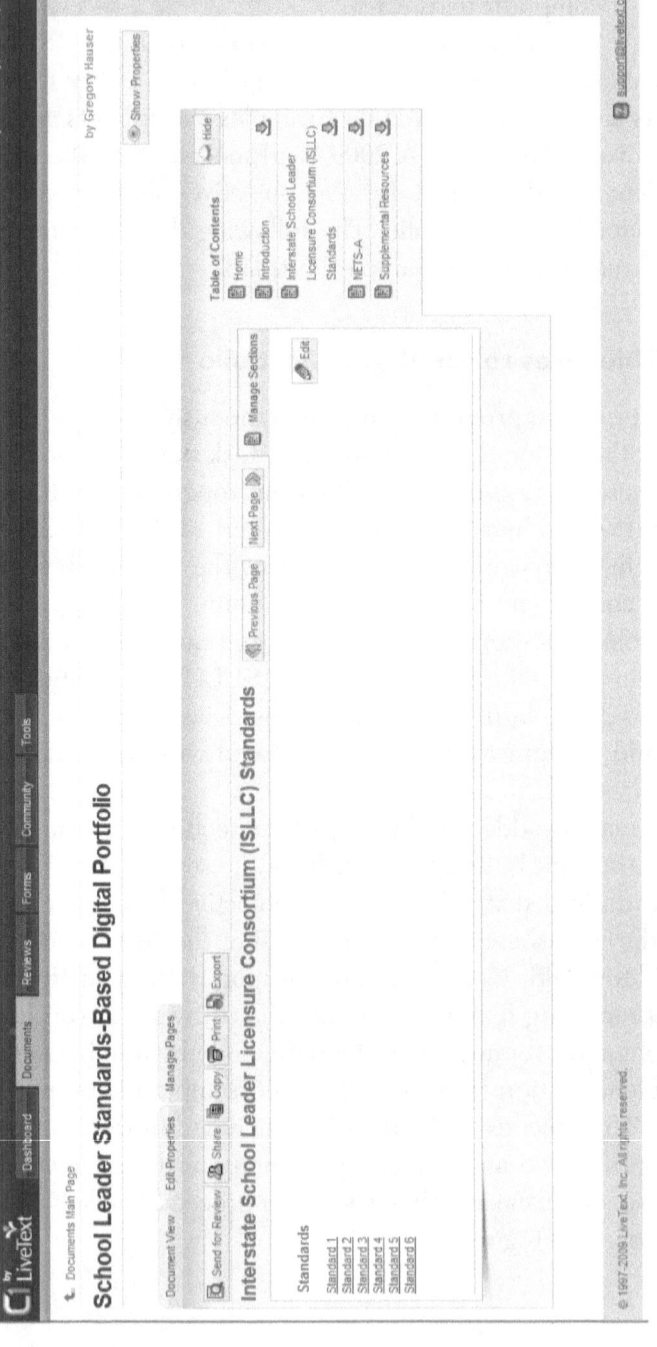

Figure 7.7. ISLLC 2008. Standards

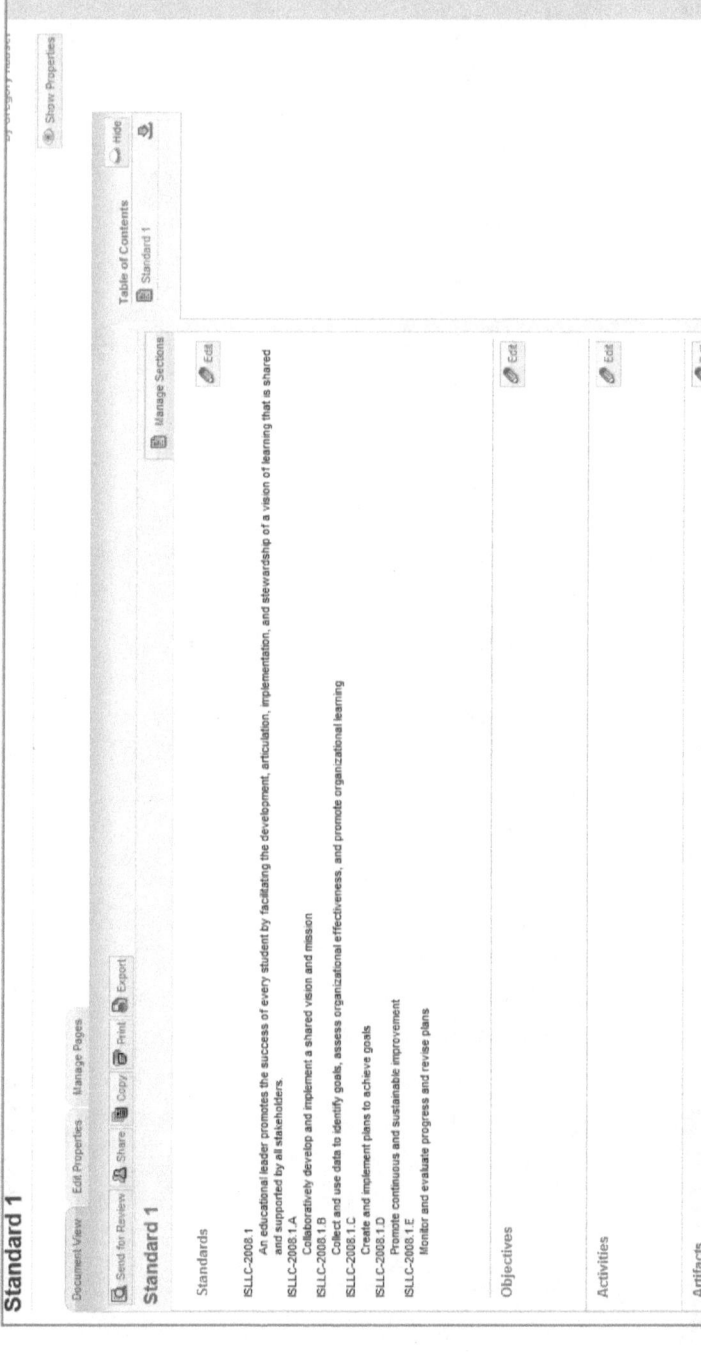

Figure 7.8. Add Content to the Objectives Section of a Standard

Figure 7.9. Adding and Saving Objectives to Portfolio

Adding Activities to the Digital Portfolio

Add the desired text related to activities associated with each objective by copying and pasting from the worksheets or by word processing the text directly into the Section Editor field. Note that you can modify the text through various word processing features built into the software. Again, if you have more than one activity for any given objective, code by numbers and letters for clear identification (see the completed sample digital portfolio for examples). The activities should all be included in the Section Editor field. Click the Save and Finish icon when you have finished adding the objective. You can save changes as you proceed by clicking the Save Changes icon. See Figure 7.10.

Adding Artifacts to the Digital Portfolio

An artifact is the evidence of what has been accomplished through the activities associated with a standard. This evidence can widely vary but typically consists of word documents, images, spreadsheets, video clips, PowerPoint presentations, and Web links. In order for artifacts to be labeled consistent with the recommended numbering and lettering system suggested in this handbook, we recommend that files first be uploaded and archived prior to adding to the artifact section of a standard. In order to accomplish this task, log on, select Tools, then File Manager, then Upload Files/Images. With the browse icon, select the pathway to the artifacts you want to upload to the File Manager. See Figure 7.11. Once documents are in the File Manager, you can rename them, if necessary, for identification in the portfolio. Use the Rename icon to the far right of a file for this purpose.

Once the File Manager has been populated with artifacts, proceed to the Artifacts Section of a standard. In order to add a document, click the Upload New File icon. Identify the file in the browser field and click the Upload file icon on the left side of the screen. See Figure 7.12.

Web links can be added in the text field of the Section Editor of an Artifacts page. You can either copy and paste the link or word process the link into the text field. The Source icon to the left and above the text field is an HTML editor that allows the addition of text from other text

Figure 7.10. Adding Activities

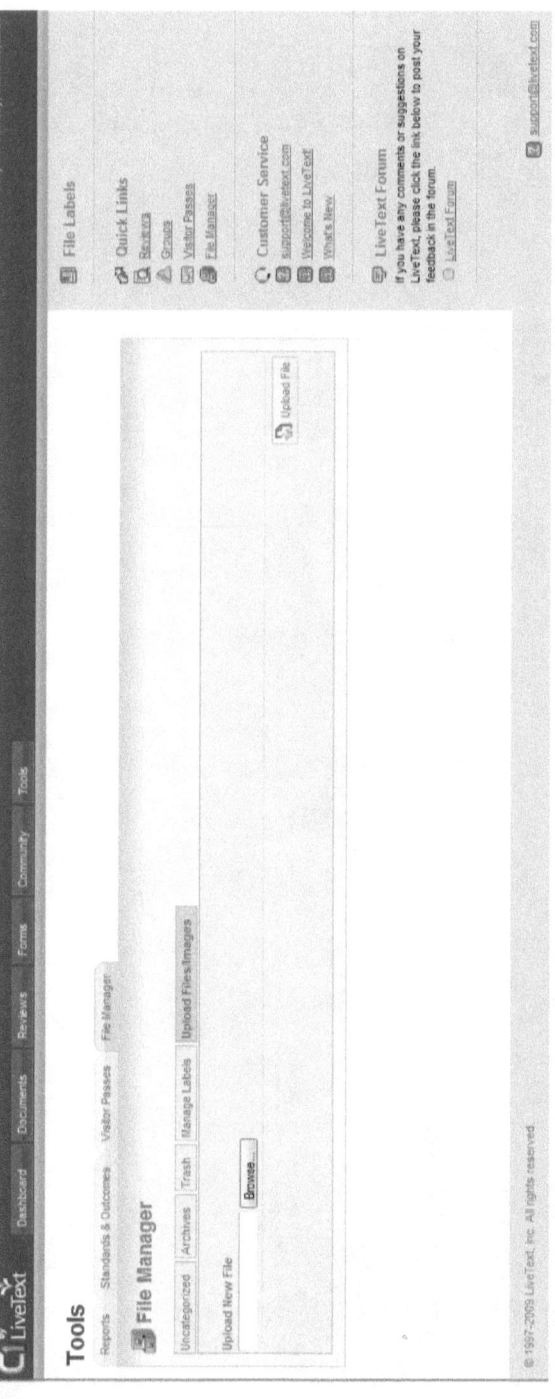

Figure 7.11. Adding Artifacts to the File Manager

Figure 7.12. Adding Files and Images to Artifact Section

editors. The editor has functions to adjust a document's layout, to insert LiveText links that lead to other LiveText documents, and to create Web links. Type a brief name for the link and then insert the Web address. To avoid typing errors in a Web address, copy and paste it into the text field.

In adding artifacts, remember that viewers often need supplemental information that indicates what they are viewing and how it relates to the selected standard, objective, and activity. Therefore, the artifacts section of each standard requires thorough planning and assembly. Refer to the sample portfolio for examples of how this might be accomplished.

ACCESS AND REVIEW OF THE SAMPLE DIGITAL PORTFOLIO

Complete the following steps to access the sample template:

1. Log on to LiveText with your username and password. See Figure 7.1.
2. From the Dashboard page click on the Documents icon in the toolbar at the top of the page. See Figure 7.3.
3. Click on the New button on the left-hand side of the lower toolbar. See Figure 7.4.
4. In the Folder field choose the Template option. In the Template field select Sample Standards-Based Digital Portfolio. See Figure 7.5.
5. Enter a Title for your standards-based digital portfolio (My Sample Portfolio).
6. Enter a Description at your discretion.
7. Click the Save a New Document button located on the lower right side below the Template Outline.

ACTIVITY

Complete the formative evaluation rubric included in the resources available on the enclosed CD or on LiveText at various times during the development process. Each time, have a critical friend complete the rubric as well. Compare and contrast these responses. Identify strengths and opportunities for improvement. Develop strategies for improvement. Identify issues and concerns and explore these with a critical friend.

SUMMARY

In this chapter, the LiveText online portfolio option was presented. The process of logging on, registering, and subscribing to LiveText is a matter of following the screen prompts. Within LiveText, you can access the standards-based school leader digital portfolio template; modify the portfolio outline; and add objectives, activities, and artifacts. You are now prepared to assemble the standards-based digital portfolio in LiveText.

8

EVALUATION OF THE STANDARDS-BASED DIGITAL SCHOOL LEADER PORTFOLIO

In this chapter, we examine why and how the digital portfolio is used to evaluate school leaders and candidates. In this way, leaders and candidates can be prepared to present their portfolios for evaluation. We also include standards-based scoring scales to determine the quality of a digital school leader portfolio.

WHY USE STANDARDS-BASED DIGITAL PORTFOLIOS TO EVALUATE SCHOOL LEADER CANDIDATES AND SCHOOL LEADERS?

There are three primary reasons why standards-based digital portfolios are useful in evaluating school leader candidates and school leaders. First, an emerging body of literature relates the frustration school leaders have with traditional forms of evaluation and the need for alternatives (Brown & Irby, 2001; Gil, 1998). According to school leaders, traditional evaluations "do not improve performance, do not promote professional growth or school improvement, do not relate to what contributes to principal effectiveness, lack clear definition of job functions, are done to them rather than for or with them, prevent adaptive responses to problems, are oriented to obsolete procedural checklists, are inconsistent and informal, and inhibit open communication and dialogue between evaluators and principals" (Brown & Irby, 2001, p. 5).

Not surprisingly, school leader preparation candidates often share these same frustrations with traditional forms of evaluation. In contrast, the digital portfolio has the potential to provide a contextual, more authentic, and more complete basis for assessing standards-based knowledge, performance, and dispositions of school leader candidates and school leaders. The digital portfolio is heralded as an assessment tool that "not only provides true and rich information for reflecting and assessing the true performance and achievement of learners, but also helps [learners] engage in meaningful learning" (Chang, 2001, p. 145).

In general, "most educators believe that the use of portfolios encourages productive changes in curriculum, instruction, and student learning" (Herman & Winters, 1994, p. 52). Despite these laudable claims, however, a review of the literature reveals a general lack of empirical research on portfolios (Carney, 2001). In particular, "relatively absent is attention to technical quality, to serious indicators of impact, or to rigorous testing of assumptions" (Herman & Winters, 1994, p. 48). Further, "little is known regarding the capacity of portfolio assessments to support judgments that are valid for large-scale [assessment purposes]" (Novak, Herman, & Gearhart, 1996, p. 2).

Although the digital portfolio is a promising and much needed alternative to other models of evaluating school leaders, further refinement and research are needed to establish the superiority of this assessment approach. We do not address these larger research concerns; however, evaluative instrumentation in the Supplemental Resources folder on TaskStream, LiveText, and at http://tiny.cc/Digital_Portfolio for those using PowerPoint provide a structured framework and a process for evaluation.

Second, school leaders and school leader candidates can demonstrate, through their example, how to use standards-based digital portfolios as both teaching and evaluative tools. "If principals are planning to advocate the use of digital portfolios with teachers and/or students, they can gain a great deal by participating in the process themselves" (Kilbane & Milman, 2003, p. 144).

Third, because you can distribute standards-based digital portfolios through e-mail or a Web link, they have the potential to facilitate greater opportunities for feedback and evaluation (Costantino & De Lorenzo, 2002). In sum, the standards-based digital portfolio provides an alternative approach to assessment of school leader and school leader candidate competence, to demonstrating leadership in the use of technology and the portfolio as an assessment tool, and to increasing greater opportunities for feedback and evaluation.

WHAT ARE THE DIFFERENT TYPES OF EVALUATION USED IN ASSESSING A STANDARDS-BASED DIGITAL PORTFOLIO?

Two common types of evaluation identified in the literature, formative and summative (Scriven, 1991), are appropriate for assessing digital portfolios. The formative evaluation occurs during the development of the standards-based digital portfolio. "The goal of formative evaluation is to determine whether the materials fulfill the intended purpose. . . . The purpose or objectives of the materials are central to this type of evaluation" (Kilbane & Milman, 2003, p. 80). The summative evaluation occurs after the completion of the standards-based digital portfolio and determines the quality of the portfolio. "Quality is usually measured by how well something compares with a certain set of standards" (Kilbane & Milman, 2003, p. 80).

HOW ARE THEY EVALUATED?

There are many different types of rubrics available to evaluate standards-based digital portfolios. Some excellent examples include those developed by Martin-Kniep (1999), Hartnell-Young and Morriss (1999), and Brown and Irby (1997). However, this text includes ten different rubrics that have been developed *specifically* for evaluation of the standards-based digital school leader portfolio:

1. ISLLC 2008 self-assessment (Perceived Importance),
2. ISLLC 2008 self-assessment (Entry Skill Level),
3. ISLLC 2008 self-assessment (Culminating Skill Level),

4. NETS-A 2009 self-assessment (Perceived Importance),
5. NETS-A 2009 self-assessment (Entry Skill Level),
6. NETS-A 2009 self-assessment (Culminating Skill Level),
7. Standards-Based Digital Portfolio Formative Evaluation,
8. Standards-Based Digital Portfolio Summative Evaluation,
9. School Leader Portfolio ISLLC 2008 Rubric (used to aggregate student data in either TaskStream or LiveText for accreditation or other purposes), and
10. School Leader Portfolio NETS-A 2009 Rubric (used to aggregate student data in either TaskStream or LiveText for accreditation or other purposes).

See the Supplemental Resources folder at http://tiny.cc/Digital_Portfolio, or access the Supplemental Resources pages on TaskStream or LiveText. The order in which these evaluation rubrics should be used is outlined in the Activities section at the end of this chapter.

There are three scales included in the ISLLC 2008 self-assessment. In the first scale, readers rank the relative importance of each element of each standard. In the second scale, readers identify their perceived entry skill level. These two self-assessments should be completed at the beginning the digital portfolio process.

In the third scale, readers identify their skill level at the end of the digital portfolio project. This self-assessment is applied differently, depending on the user. For example, school leaders find their reflection on these scales useful in developing professional development activities, whereas school leader candidates find their reflection on these scales useful in developing the internship experience. Given the depth of the ISLLC 2008 Standards, this self-assessment provides focus and a rich source of information for planning and reflection.

Similarly, the NETS-A 2009 technology self-assessment should be completed at the beginning and at the end of the digital portfolio process. Like the ISLLC 2008 self-assessment, the NETS-A 2009 self-assessment is applied differently by school leaders, school leader candidates, and school leadership faculty. Using the same three scales used in the ISLLC 2008 self-assessment, readers identify the perceived importance of each element of the NETS-A 2009 Standards, their perceived skill level at the beginning of the digital portfolio project, and their culminating skill level at the end of the project.

The NETS-A 2009 self-assessment may also be valuable if you have a choice of digital portfolio formats. Use the formative assessment rubric to evaluate your work or share it with a critical friend to receive feedback. The formative assessment rubric is designed to guide reflective assessment while the portfolio is developed. School leaders and school leader candidates benefit from using this instrument at various stages in the development of the digital portfolio. A supervisor or school leadership faculty member can use the summative assessment rubric to evaluate a school leader or a school leader candidate's digital portfolio. These are representative samples of appropriate rubrics; however, other rubrics could also be used.

WHO CONDUCTS THE EVALUATION?

The evaluation should include the individual who constructed the portfolio, critical friends, and others, depending on the constituency, content, and purpose of the standards-based portfolio. Revisit Chapter 1 for aspects of these three factors. For school leader candidates, evaluations include the candidate, school leadership preparation faculty, critical friends, and perhaps site supervisors. Evaluations for school leaders include the portfolio creator, supervisors, peers, and others who can contribute informed feedback.

ACTIVITIES

At the beginning of the development of the digital portfolio:

- Complete the perceived importance and the entry skill level scales of the ISLLC 2008 self-assessment. Compare and contrast the responses related to these two scales. Give particular attention to those elements considered very important and that have the lowest entry skill level.
- Complete the perceived importance and the entry skill level scales of the NETS-A 2009 self-assessment. Compare and contrast the responses related to these two scales. Give particular attention to those elements considered very important and that have the lowest entry skill level.

During the development of the digital portfolio:

Complete the Formative Evaluation Instrument at various stages in the development of the digital portfolio. Have a critical friend complete the Formative Evaluation Instrument at the same time. Compare and contrast these responses. Identify strengths as well as opportunities for improvement. Develop strategies to address opportunities for improvement.

At the conclusion of the digital portfolio:

Complete the culminating skill level scale for both the ISLLC 2008 self-assessment and the NETS-A 2009 self-assessment. Compare and contrast these responses with the responses related to the perceived importance and the entry skill level of each element of the standards. Identify elements that are perceived as areas of strength and elements that present opportunities for continued growth.

The summative assessment rubric may be used by a supervisor or educational leadership faculty member to evaluate a school leader or a school leader candidate's digital portfolio. College and university faculty may use the School Leader Portfolio ISLLC 2008 Rubric and the School Leader Portfolio NETS-A 2009 Rubric for aggregating data across students for accreditation or programmatic improvement.

SUMMARY

This chapter provided a brief overview of the types, purposes, and methods of evaluation of the standards-based digital portfolio. Instrumentation to be used in the evaluation of the standards-based digital portfolio was introduced for use by readers for both formative and summative purposes.

REFERENCES

Arter, J. A. (1992, April). *Portfolios in practice: What is a portfolio?* Paper presented at the annual meeting of the American Educational Research Association, San Francisco, CA.

Baltimore, M., Hickson, J., George, J. D., & Crutchfield, L. B. (1996). Portfolio assessment: A model for counselor education. *Counselor Education and Supervision, 36*(2), 113–121.

Barrett, H. C. (1998). Strategic questions: What to consider when planning for electronic portfolios. *Learning and Leading with Technology, 26*(2), 6–13.

Barrett, H. C. (2000). Create your own electronic portfolio using off-the-shelf software to showcase your own or student work. *Learning and Leading with Technology, 27*(7), 14–21.

Brown, G., & Irby, B. J. (1997). *The principal portfolio.* Thousand Oaks, CA: Crown.

Brown, G., & Irby, B. J. (2001). *The principal portfolio* (2nd ed.). Thousand Oaks, CA: Sage.

Capasso, R. L., & Daresh, J. C. (2001). *The school administrator internship handbook; Leading, mentoring, and participating in the internship program.* Thousand Oaks, CA: Corwin.

Carney, J. (2001). Electronic and traditional portfolios as tools for teacher knowledge representation. *Dissertation Abstracts International, 62*(05A), 1798–2065.

Chang, C. (2001). Construction and evaluation of a Web-based learning portfolio system: An electronic assessment tool. *Innovations in Education and Teaching International, 38*(2), 144–155.

Chirichello, M. (2001). Collective leadership: Sharing the principalship. *Principal, 81*(1), 46–51.

Constantino, P. M., & De Lorenzo, M. N. (2002). *Developing a professional teaching portfolio; A guide for success.* Boston: Allyn & Bacon.

Council of Chief State School Officers. (1996). *Interstate school leader licensure consortium: Standards for school leaders.* Washington, DC. Retrieved May 8, 2010, from http://www.ccsso.org/content/pdfs/isllcstd.pdf

Council of Chief State School Officers. (2008). *Educational Leadership Policy Standards: ISLLC 2008 as adopted by the National Policy Board for Educational Administration.* Washington, DC. Retrieved May 8, 2010, from http://www.ccsso.org/content/pdfs/elps_isllc2008.pdf

Creighton, T. (2003). *The principal as technology leader.* Thousand Oaks, CA: Corwin.

Cruz, J. (1998). Continuous learning. *Thrust for Educational Leadership, 27*(7), 32–25.

Dewey, J. (1933). *How we think; A restatement of the relation of reflective thinking to the educative process.* Boston: Heath.

Flanagan, L., & Jacobsen, M. (2003). Technology leadership for the twenty-first century principal. *Journal of Educational Administration, 41*(2), 124–142.

Freire, P. (1973). *Pedagogy of the oppressed.* New York: Seabury Press.

Gil, L. (1998, October). Principals evaluating peers. *School Administrator, 55*(99), 28–30.

Giroux, H. A. (2001). *Theory and resistance in education; Towards a pedagogy for the opposition.* Westport, CT: Bergin & Garvey.

Gosmire, D., & Grady, M. L. (2007). A bumpy road: Principal as technology leader. *Principal Leadership* (Middle School Edition), 7(6), 16–21.

Gray, L., & Lewis, L. (2009). *Educational technology in public school districts: Fall 2008* (NCES 2010–003). Washington, DC: National Center for Education Statistics, Institute of Education Sciences, U.S. Department of Education.

Hackmann, D. G., Schmitt-Oliver, D. M., & Tracy, J. C. (2002). *The standards-based administrative internship: Putting the ISLLC standards into practice.* Lanham, MD: Scarecrow Press.

Hale, E. L., & Moorman, H. N. (2003). *Preparing school principals: A national perspective on policy and program innovations.* Institute for Educational Leadership, Washington, DC: and Edwardsville, IL: Illinois Education Research Council.

Hartnell-Young, E., & Morriss, M. (1999). *Digital professional portfolios for change.* Arlington Heights, IL: Skylight.

Hauser, G. M., & Koutouzos, D. W. (2005). *The standards-based digital school leader portfolio; A handbook for preparation and practice.* Lanham, MD: Rowman & Littlefield.

REFERENCES

Hauser, G. M., & Koutouzos, D. W. (2009). Technology training and professional development of school leaders in the U.S.A.: The critical need for reform. In I. M. Saleh & M. S. Khine (Eds.), *Transformational leadership and educational excellence: Learning organizations in the information age* (pp. 245–265). Rotterdam: Sense Publishers B.V.

Hauser, G. M., Koutouzos, D. W., & Olson, G. E. (2005). The standards-based school leader digital portfolio: A case study of student perceptions. *International Journal of Learning, 12*(7), 311–316.

Herman, J., & Winters, L. (1994). Portfolio research: A slim collection. *Educational Leadership, 52*(2), 48–56.

International Society for Technology in Education. (2009). *National technology standards and performance indicators for administrators*. Retrieved May 8, 2010, from http://www.iste.org/Content/NavigationMenu/NETS/ForAdministrators/2009Standards/NETS-A_2009.pdf

Jones, B. F., Valdez, G., Nowakowski, J., & Rasmussen, C. (1999). *Plugging in; Choosing and using educational technology*. Washington, DC: NEKIA Communications.

Katz, M. S., Noddings, N., & Strike, K. A. (Eds.). (1999). *Justice and caring; The search for common ground in education*. New York: Teachers College Press.

Kilbane, C. R., & Milman, N. B. (2003). *The digital teaching portfolio handbook; A how-to guide for educators*. New York: Allyn & Bacon.

Kleiner, B., Thomas, N., & Lewis, L. (2007). *Educational technology in teacher education programs for initial licensure* (NCES 2008–040). National Center for Education Statistics, Institute of Education Sciences, U.S. Department of Education. Washington, DC.

Lackney, J. A. (2005). New approaches for school design. In F. W. English (Ed.), *The Sage handbook of educational leadership: Advances in theory, research, and practice* (pp. 506–537). Thousand Oaks, CA: Sage.

Lenhart, A. (2009). *Teens and sexting*. Washington, DC: Pew Internet and American Life Project, Pew Research Center.

Levine, A. (2005). *Educating school leaders*. Washington, DC: Education Schools Project.

Lombardi, J. (2008). To portfolio or not to portfolio: Helpful or hyped? *College Teaching, 56*(1), 7–10.

Marcoux, J., Brown, G., Irby, B. J., & Lara-Alecio, R. (2003, April). *A case study on the use of portfolios in principal evaluation*. Paper presented at the annual meeting of the American Educational Research Association. Chicago.

Martin, G. E., Wright, W. F., & Danzig, A. B. (2003). *School leader internship; Developing, monitoring, and evaluating your leadership experience*. Larchmont, NY: Eye on Education.

Martin-Kniep, G. O. (1999). *Capturing the wisdom of practice*. Washington, DC: ASCD.

McNabb, M. L. (2006). Portable data empowers leaders: A training program for administrators in Michigan encourages a leadership infrastructure for school improvement through handheld technology. *Learning and Leading with Technology: The ISTE Journal of Educational Technology Practice and Policy, 33*(8), 24–28.

Meadows, R. B., & Dyal, A. B.,& Wright (1999). Implementing portfolio assessment in the development of school administrators: Improving preparation for educational leadership. *Education, 120*(2), 304–14.

Means, B. (2001). Technology use in tomorrow's schools. *Educational Leadership: Journal of the Association of Supervision and Curriculum Development, NEA, 58*(4), 57–62.

Metropolitan Planning Council. (2002). *Education technology; Developing an educational technology agenda for Illinois*. Chicago: Author.

Montgomery, K., & Wiley, D. (2004). *Creating e-portfolios using PowerPoint; A guide for educators*. Thousand Oaks, CA: Sage.

Montgomery, K., & Wiley, D. (2008). *Building e-portfolios using PowerPoint: A guide for educators*. Thousand Oaks, CA: Sage.

Murphy, J. (2003, September). *Reculturing educational leadership: The ISLLC standards ten years out*. Paper presented to the National Policy Board for Educational Administration. Reston, VA.

National Commission for Excellence in Education. (1983). *A nation at risk: The imperative for educational reform*. Washington, DC: U.S. Government Printing Office.

National Policy Board for Educational Administration. (2002). *Standards for advanced programs in educational leadership for principals, superintendents, curriculum directors, and supervisors*. Retrieved May 8, 2010, from http://www.npbea.org/ELCC/ELCCStandards%20_5-02.pdf

National School Boards Association. (2007). *Creating and connecting; Research and guidelines on online social—and educational—networking*. Retrieved on May 8, 2010, from www.nsba.org/SecondaryMenu/TLN?CreatomgamdCpmmectomg/aspx

Newmann, F. M., Marks, H. M., & Gamoran, A. (1996). Authentic pedagogy and student performance. *American Journal of Education, 104*, 280–312.

Niguidula, D. (1997). Picturing performance with digital portfolios. *Educational Leadership, 55*(3), 26–28.

Noddings, N. (1984). *Caring: A feminine approach to ethics and moral education*. Berkeley: University of California Press.

Novak, J. R., Herman, J. L., & Gearhart, M. (1996). Issues in portfolio assessment: The scoreability of narrative collections (CSE Technical Report No. 410). Los Angeles, CA: National Center for Research on Evaluation, Standards, and Student Testing assessments in large-scale testing programs. *Educational Evaluation and Policy Analysis, 19*(1), 1–14.

REFERENCES

Schon, D. A. (1983). *The reflective practitioner: How professionals think in action.* New York: Basic Books.

Scriven, M. (1991). Beyond formative and summative evaluation. In M. W. McLaughlin & D. C. Phillips (Eds.), *Evaluation and education: At quarter century* (pp. 19–64). Chicago: University of Chicago Press.

Sheingold, K. (1992). *Technology and assessment.* Paper presented at Technology and School Reform Conference, Dallas, TX.

TSSA Collaborative. (2001). *Technology Standards for School Administrators* (TSSA). Retrieved May 8, 2010, from http://www.ncrtec.org/pd/tssa/

Valli, L. (1997). Listening to other voices: A description of teacher reflection in the United States. *Peabody Journal of Education, 72*(1), 67–88.

Wells, J., & Lewis, L. (2006). *Internet access in U.S. public schools and classrooms: 1994–2005* (NCES 2007-020). U.S. Department of Education. Washington, DC: National Center for Education Statistics.

Wiggins, G. P. (1989). A true test: Toward more authentic and equitable assessment. *Phi Delta Kappan, 70*, 703–713.

Wildy, H., & Wallace, J. (1998). Professionalism, portfolios and the development of school leaders. *School Leadership & Management, 18*(1), 123–141.

Wolf, K., & Siu-Runyon, Y. (1996). Portfolio purposes and possibilities. *Journal of Adolescent and Adult Literacy, 40*(1), 30–37.

Yerkes, D. M., & Guaglianone, C. L. (1998). The administrative portfolio. *Thrust for Educational Leadership, 27*(7), 28–32.

Zandberg, I., & Lewis, L. (2008). *Technology-based distance education courses for public elementary and secondary school students: 2002–03 and 2004–05* (NCES 2008–008). National Center for Education Statistics, Institute of Education Sciences, U.S. Department of Education. Washington, DC.

ABOUT THE AUTHORS

Gregory M. Hauser is associate professor in the Department of Educational Leadership at Roosevelt University. He currently teaches the following courses: internship, education foundations, and politics and educational policy. Dr. Hauser's research interests include school reform, technology in education, and comparative education. As an outgrowth of his interest in comparative education, he completed a Fulbright Scholarship to Germany. He serves on the editorial board for the Journal of Scholarship and Practice and the International Online Journal of Educational Sciences. Prior to his role as a faculty member, he served for seventeen years as a chief student affairs officer, most recently as vice provost for student affairs at Roosevelt University. He received a Ph.D. in educational administration from the University of Wisconsin–Madison.

Dennis Koutouzos served as assistant to the dean of the College of Education at Roosevelt University and has since retired. Following a career as a high school English teacher, he served as technology coordinator at the South Cook Educational Service Center, where he helped design and implement the State of Illinois technology initiatives. At Roosevelt University, he redesigned and taught a course for teachers, Technology in the Classroom, planned and implemented the technology lab for the College of Education, and served on University technology committees. Mr. Koutouzos serves on the Board of Examiners for the National Council for the Accreditation of Teacher Education (NCATE).

www.ingramcontent.com/pod-product-compliance
Lightning Source LLC
Chambersburg PA
CBHW022015300426
44117CB00005B/208